BECOME UNMISTAKABLE

BECOME
UNMISTAKABLE

START THE JOURNEY FROM COMMODITY TO ODDITY

MICHAEL D. NOVAKOSKI
WITH JOHN M. PARKER

Advantage®

Published by Advantage, Charleston, South Carolina.
Member of Advantage Media Group.

ADVANTAGE is a registered trademark, and the Advantage colophon is a trademark of Advantage Media Group, Inc.

Printed in the United States of America.

10 9 8 7 6 5 4 3 2

ISBN: 978-1-59932-915-4
LCCN: 2018937759

Cover design by Melanie Cloth.
Layout design by Megan Elger.

This publication is designed to provide accurate and authoritative information in regard to the subject matter covered. It is sold with the understanding that the publisher is not engaged in rendering legal, accounting, or other professional services. If legal advice or other expert assistance is required, the services of a competent professional person should be sought.

Advantage Media Group is proud to be a part of the Tree Neutral® program. Tree Neutral offsets the number of trees consumed in the production and printing of this book by taking proactive steps such as planting trees in direct proportion to the number of trees used to print books. To learn more about Tree Neutral, please visit **www.treeneutral.com**.

Advantage Media Group is a publisher of business, self-improvement, and professional development books and online learning. We help entrepreneurs, business leaders, and professionals share their Stories, Passion, and Knowledge to help others Learn & Grow. Do you have a manuscript or book idea that you would like us to consider for publishing? Please visit **advantagefamily.com** or call **1.866.775.1696**.

To those who walked alongside us, supporting the creation, exploration, and blazing of new trails.

TABLE OF CONTENTS

ACKNOWLEDGMENTS

Many people have played essential roles in the cultural journey that shaped this book. First, we want to acknowledge our wives, Liz Novakoski and Mary Parker, for their seemingly limitless patience and support as we pursue our passion for "becoming the best version of ourselves" and creating the "best version of our company" for our team members. Thank you both for serving in your roles as CEOs of multiple "little start-ups" (our combined six children). Your leadership in the development of our families inside the home is crucial to the successful balance of life, as we so often work outside the home far more days than you would like.

Thank you to our executive team, the true integrators of our vision for right-brained leadership and employee-centric culture. We are privileged to call Joe Novakoski, Tony Roussey, and Grace Silva friends and partners in our endeavors; without them there would be no book to write. We would also like to extend our gratitude to the Novakoski, Roussey, and Silva families for their encouragement and support.

Thank you to Mike King, who led Elzinga & Volkers from the mid-1990s to the late 2000s. Your left-brained leadership set us on a solid financial and operational foundation from which to jump off on our cultural journey.

Special thanks to Morgan Weaver and Rachel Austin for their direct assistance with this book and the many hours of logistical support, which kept us on track and on schedule. Thank you to the Elzinga & Volkers marketing team for your hard work supporting our speaking engagements and visual communication tools. Thank you to the field and office leadership teams at Elzinga & Volkers, collectively known as our leadership council. Your insights, inspiration, and constructive criticism add color to our corporate culture in a world of black and white.

Thank you to the thousands of employees of Elzinga & Volkers. Over a span of seventy-two years, each of you, past and present, have had a tremendous impact on our business and community. Those of you who work alongside us now have enriched our lives and inspired the concepts in this book.

From Mike: I would like to thank the members of YPO – MI-6, my Construction Industry Forum, and fellow International Forum Committee members. The value of YPO in my personal and profession life extends far beyond what I can put into words. A special thank you to all the mentors, sponsors, coaches, and "Yodas" who have left a lasting imprint on us; I especially acknowledge my friend, Ed H., and the life-changing program developed by Dr. Bob and Bill W. that so many of my dear friends are associated with. I am living "The Promises."

To those we may have missed—friends, clients, trade partners, and respected competitors—we offer our sincere thanks and gratitude for all you have taught us and for your support. Each person, each victory, and each challenge shapes our leadership styles and inspire the concepts in this book.

Lastly, and most importantly, we thank God for making all things possible and showing us His will to act upon.

ABOUT THE AUTHORS

ABOUT MIKE NOVAKOSKI

Mike Novakoski is the president and CEO of national-award-winning Elzinga & Volkers Construction Professionals (E&V), the EV Group, and Become Unmistakable Consulting. At this writing, Mike has thirty years of construction industry experience and a special gift for innovative thinking, visioning, communication, and motivation in his organizational leadership roles. In addition to authoring two books, Mike is a nationally recognized speaker on the subjects of "six-pack abs" culture, the power of VisCom (visual communication), breaking out of the commodity mind-sct, innovation at all levels, and "right-brain-justified" leadership.

Mike has been a member of the Young Presidents Organization (YPO) since 2007. After serving as an officer on chapter and regional levels, he was elected to serve on the International Forum Committee of this 25,000-plus member organization. YPO often calls on Mike's expertise for global training, assisting in the development of new organization-wide programs, publishing articles and videos, and speaking at international events to inspire thousands of other CEOs.

Mike is a lifelong learner who holds a BS in construction management, an MBA with an emphasis in finance, and an Innovation Management certification. He wrote this book while participating in a three-year Harvard Business School Owner/President Management program. Mike also does a considerable amount of public speaking each year—his audiences including both for-profit and nonprofit organizations in a variety of industries, both nationally and internationally.

Mike has been married to his wife, Liz, since 1996. They have four children—Noah, Madison, Faith, and KT—and reside in western Michigan.

ABOUT JOHN PARKER

John has served alongside Mike and two other partners at Elzinga & Volkers Construction Professionals since he completed an undergraduate degree in facilities management. John has also earned his master's degree in business administration as well as an Innovation Management certification.

John is passionate about team building and leading change in organizational management. He spends most of his days leading project teams through the early stages of project development, and occasionally joins Mike in public-speaking engagements and leadership consulting. John lives in western Michigan with his wife, Mary, and their two daughters, Macy and Ellison.

ABOUT ELZINGA & VOLKERS CONSTRUCTION PROFESSIONALS

Founded in 1945, Elzinga & Volkers Construction Professionals (E&V) is a leading provider of construction services. Based in western Michigan, E&V works nationally and employs more than two hundred team members. As of this writing, E&V has received eight Elite Awards as a West Michigan Best and Brightest Company to Work For; it has also been recognized as a National Best and Brightest firm for each year of the program's existence, taking home two Elite Awards. E&V has received the Michigan Contractor of the Year award twice since 2012 and was recently honored with the prestigious West Coast Chamber's Business Leadership Award. Associated Builders and Contractors, a 21,000-member trade organization, awarded E&V one of its top national safety awards in 2018. Elzinga & Volkers is a leader on all levels—notably in construction safety—having recently celebrated ten years with no lost-time incidents, exemplifying its dedication to an employee-centric culture that puts people before profit.

FOREWORD

Everyone wants to know: How do you create an extraordinary company?

In *Become Unmistakable*, Mike Novakoski and John Parker lay bare how Elzinga & Volkers grew from a small construction firm in western Michigan to an award-winning, nationally known company that is in high demand by clients and as a place to work. Mike and his colleagues engineered this transformation by putting people—the very people who create value for the organization—first. When you read this honest and inspiring book you will see that it is not just tech companies that create value by treating people right. This approach can be used in any industry, even one where people get dirty every day.

One of the most important things Mike has done at Elzinga & Volkers is to change how colleagues treat each other. This starts with language. To call someone a "subcontractor" signals that they are below others and therefore less important. Elzinga & Volkers began calling these skilled professionals "trade contractors," putting them on an equal footing with general contractors and other professionals on worksites. The construction industry, as the book reports, is beginning to follow their lead and adopt this designation for tradespeople.

Another telling language choice at Elzinga & Volkers is the use of "unmistakably" in their projects. They want their clients to know that they are special and different, that there is something unmistakably Elzinga & Volkers in their work. This is not just good marketing; it is the product of a broader philosophy that puts people first.

By focusing on safety as the number-one priority at E&V construction sites, Mike and his team signal that taking risks and getting hurt to meet a deadline or budget is simply not acceptable. One part of this commitment to care for those who work for them is that they offer safety-training courses at no cost not only to their staff, but to the tradespeople who work on a per-project basis. This strongly demonstrates that people come first.

In turn, everyone at Elzinga & Volkers puts in the extra effort that has made it a premier builder. People line up to work for them, and those who are hired enjoy being part of their organization—part of the Elzinga & Volkers family, Mike would say. The book describes the important "little things" that remind colleagues that they are a family, including personal Christmas gifts and letters from Mike—not just to the employee, but to his or her family as well. In fact, the book describes how colleagues' families are included in celebrations at work. Mike reports that one of his best success metrics is when spouses spontaneously tell him that their families are happier because the employee loves what he or she is doing and is treated like a professional. Happy employees are inevitably happier spouses, parents, and citizens.

But it goes farther than that. Mike is clear that his Christian values infuse how he runs his business. He believes he has an obligation to bring compassion and love to work so that people know that values are their most important asset. This is not only an important moral approach; the book makes clear that it is smart business. Elzinga & Volkers is unmistakably profitable, because people want to give their utmost effort to support each other and ultimately "wow" their clients. *Become Unmistakable* not only outlines the successes

Mike's approach has produced, but also goes through the mistakes they have made and what they have learned from them.

You will see the gears moving by reading *Become Unmistakable*. It's not always pretty, but Mike and his team have made revolutionary changes at Elzinga & Volkers that have transformed their industry. If they can do it, then you can transform your organization, too, whatever industry you're in, whether for-profit or nonprofit. It's time to become *unmistakable*.

Paul J. Zak, PhD
Author of *Trust Factor: The Science of Creating High-Performance Companies*

INTRODUCTION

I grew up as a raving fan of *The Wizard of Oz*. I would watch the 1939 film on television each Easter Sunday and really connect to the different characters. Watching the journey that Dorothy took with the Lion, the Scarecrow, and the Tin Man, I couldn't help but focus on her underlying misery. I saw Dorothy's sadness about her life as she sat on her farm in the Kansas dust bowl. Only "somewhere over the rainbow" could her dreams come true. But she also had a belief that she could attain something more in life, that one day she would get there.

And then Dorothy decides to run away. The twister comes. She's accidentally knocked unconscious, and the house goes up in the air, spinning around. The movie is in stark black and white, and there's a foreshadowing of the Wicked Witch. Dorothy's house is spinning, and it hits the ground with a loud thump, followed by total silence. She walks slowly to the door. You see just the door handle and Dorothy's hand reaching out for it. She turns it slowly. As she's opening the door, she moves out of the way to reveal a full view of a scene in Technicolor.

Technicolor was a big deal in the filming technology of 1939, and a perfect expression of the amazing life journey that Dorothy was beginning.

At this point, Dorothy is looking out into Munchkinland, where her house has landed on the Wicked Witch of the East, killing her—to the gratitude of the Munchkins. She is beginning an exciting journey, meeting new characters, and facing and solving challenges together with them. The important thing is that she is okay being lost because she is with these partners on her fantastic journey. That's why the emotional farewell that she has with them is so memorable. As you may recall, she finds the wizard is just a magician from Kansas who got caught up in the same storm—but who also has a hot air balloon, and who says he can get her back to Kansas. Before they launch the balloon, she says goodbye to her three relatively new friends. She gets to the Scarecrow last, and says in a crackling voice, "I think I'm going to miss you most of all," and gives him a hug.

Whatever that scene meant to me as a child, it has taken on a new meaning in a business context. The dust bowl of Kansas, the grim black and white world, represents the life of most workers who can't wait to punch out. They are always looking forward to the weekends and dread coming back into work on Mondays. On the way home from work, they buy a lottery ticket, so they can have a chance at Oz.

> *As you say your goodbyes to everybody, your voice is cracking and you're giving hugs, and your tears flow because you don't want this work life to end. You love these people.*

At our company, we expect our front door to open into a colorful world like Oz, with lots of excitement, great stories, bonding, and shared memories. We expect to solve big challenges together as a team, so our work life is like living a dream. The kind of dream where, suddenly, you realize forty years have passed and it's time to retire. As you say your goodbyes to everybody, your voice is cracking and you're giving hugs, and your tears flow because you don't want this work life to end. You love these people.

In this book, you'll learn how our Michigan construction company got to that vision. Elzinga & Volkers became **unmistakably** different in an industry that is generally very set in its ways. Our company culture puts people before profits, and we have a thriving business with a unique model that has provided inspiration to others seeking our advice from around the world. We want to show you how right-brained leadership brought us Technicolor success!

> *The pages ahead will explain how and why we came to brand our company **Unmistakably** Elzinga & Volkers.*

Right-brained thinking, or operating "from the heart," will be explained further in chapters 1 and 2. A lot of businesses rely on left-brained leadership, watching numbers, cutting costs, seeking the lowest price. Instead, we have emphasized right-brained leadership in our business, which leads to an employee-centric culture. We'll explain that concept further in chapter 6, but, essentially, it's about creating a company culture that values treating people right, starting with how we treat our employees. We believe having happy, engaged, and empowered employees will naturally make for happy clients, repeat customers, and a better business overall. We also believe that chasing dollars and competing on price has created a commodity mind-set in our industry, further explained in chapter 7. A company whose leaders operate from the right brain will perform quality work and be awarded contracts without necessarily offering the lowest price. This attitude creates a magnetic atmosphere that others want to be a part of. Some clients will choose to pay a premium for our services because of the value that our behavior creates.

We've had many opportunities to speak to business groups about what we're doing. Audiences have connected with our vision of Oz and asked for more details, which prompted this book. It is the easiest way for us to reach the most people to inspire what we hope will be a broad shift in approach for any business, whether nonprofit or for-profit. We love speaking in public and consulting with other business leaders about our success, but we have a company to run!

"We" refers to co-authors, Mike Novakoski, CEO of Elzinga & Volkers, and John Parker, vice president of project development at Elzinga & Volkers. We are the public face of our company when it comes to activities such as making conference presentations and addressing civic groups. But our leadership style is inclusive, so generally we also are speaking for our entire executive team right on down to the newest employee. Sharing what we have learned is part of our company culture, and speaking for ourselves, we can say it's also part of our Christian principles. Whatever higher power you believe in, or whether you are atheist or agnostic, we feel our approach to business relationships can and will benefit you. We feel blessed, and believe it honors God to share our wealth and that our successful ideas are good things we have that we should not be keeping to ourselves. We also believe in respecting the privacy of those we work with, so in some cases we have withheld names or other identifying details in stories about our colleagues.

Mike Reflecting on Hiring John

John joined Elzinga & Volkers as an assistant project manager in 2005 at age twenty-one, right out of college. When I interviewed him, you would have thought he had ten years of experience in how he carried himself. John rose very quickly up the ladder because he understood what we were trying to create. He didn't sit back and enjoy the ride. He drove. He was part of the development of a lot of our innovations. John has an artistic sense that helped us deliver our message through visual, graphic communications. During presentations, when my talk gets touchy-feely, John will bring up facts and figures and explain our situation in a way that left-brained people can understand better.

John and I play off each other well. A lot of CEOs surround themselves with bobble-headed people who say, "Yes boss, whatever you say." John's not afraid to disagree and offer alternatives. That healthy conflict is something I've always valued.

The ideas presented in this book were developed over more than a dozen years. Sometimes by reading business books and attending educational events. For example, we first heard the term "right-brained" applied to business leadership in a management-innovation program only a few years before writing this book. The instructor showed a slide of a bald head with a big, metal toggle switch on top.

"Our goal for the next thirty weeks," he said, "is to teach you the value of what's on each side of this toggle switch, and to lubricate this switch so each day you can toggle between right and left brain when appropriate." We had an "aha moment," realizing that our defining characteristic, which set us apart as managers in a left-brained business world, was the right-brained leadership we had developed.

It's worth noting that we came to this realization while working as general contractors. The prevailing view in our construction industry is that business simply rises and falls with the economy.

When the economy is down, contractors lower their prices, and only when there's a boom in business do they worry about keeping their people happy, paying them a bit more so they'll stay. Our view is more introspective, believing we have control of our business, and not blaming outside forces.

We found that the way we were breaking out of the commodity mind-set in the construction industry was unique and of enough interest that we should share it. As our message resonated and we were invited to speak to bigger and bigger groups it became clear that we had developed simple, logical ways of doing business that could apply to any employer. We continued to be validated by people asking us to consult for their non-construction-related businesses, as well as by winning both local and national awards for what we do. Our hope is that at least some employers who are mistreating their people may realize the error of their ways and make a course correction that will benefit their businesses. That seems idealistic, but when we speak about these ideas we see audience members leaning forward in their seats, smiling and nodding their heads. They come up afterward eager to talk about what we are doing; one woman even asked for a hug.

The affirmation gives us faith in our philosophy and nurtures our souls. The challenge of applying our philosophy to different businesses hones our thoughts and helps us improve our programs for our people. As another benefit, we hope to chip away at negative stereotypes of the construction industry, which tends to have more of a reputation for crudeness than civility and professionalism. The fact is that general contractors we meet from around the world through professional organizations are complimentary and accepting of what we are doing. They understand that their industry requires the right resources, and with talent at a premium, not having the right people is their big constraint.

You may be questioning whether you are in a position to benefit from this book. So, let's get several things out of the way:

- We are telling our story from the viewpoint of a privately owned construction company but are speaking to all industries, nonprofit and for-profit, including those at public companies responsible to shareholders. A lot of what we do has nothing to do with spending money. And it is not aimed at any particular demographic or generation. Even a sole proprietor can benefit from our approach, because it's all about relationships.

- We employ about two hundred people. You may wonder if our experiences apply to organizations with tens of thousands of people. The practices described in this book are based on simply treating people right, a concept that can be applied to groups large and small. If you are from a large organization, try to think about these concepts as they apply to the people right around you, a project team that you are part of, or a specific division of your company. If you are the leader of a large organization, think about how you can affect the group of leaders who report directly to you. The bottom line is that your behaviors as a leader will influence others to make changes throughout the organization, no matter the size.

- It doesn't take a Harvard MBA to implement what's in this book, because it's mostly common-sense, golden rule stuff once you look at it from a right-brained, human perspective.

- If you are a left-brained manager, an engineer or a numbers person, for example, our philosophy may be more of a challenge. But if you can be open to thinking about emotion-based people skills, you'll have a great opportunity to look at yourself differently and discover new strengths and powers. We know you like data and concrete results, so we'll offer you proof of concept.

- Those who enjoy building teams and continuously learning will get great benefit.

- The charismatic, humble, and giving servant/leader will have the easiest time with our approach. If that's you, maybe you don't *need* this book—but will find it provides validation and new ideas.

You also may be wondering whether we are worried about helping our competition get better by sharing our story. When you feel humble and grateful for what you have, as we do, you know that the way to remain that way is to give away what you have. This is a Christian principle, but we'll be showing through our stories in this book how it is also a sound and proven business principle.

Most business owners think they are providing a great place to work, and they use the term "family" pretty loosely to describe their workforce. When I started at Elzinga & Volkers as an estimator in 1988, it was more Kansas than Oz, more black-and-white than Technicolor. I got into leadership of a company that was performing in an average way at best. With some bravado, or perhaps to impress shareholders, the company's leadership team listed "being the best contractor in West Michigan" in its business plan. We had no idea how or if the company could get there.

With about two hundred employees, Elzinga & Volkers is the kind of general contractor that can work nationwide on large projects, not skyscrapers but buildings well-known in their region. Our job is to look at the architect's drawings and put together all the resources necessary to complete a construction project. It could be new construction, renovations, or additions.

We are very good at managing construction in highly regulated industries, such as health care, senior living, and food and beverage. Imagine a hospital needs a complex renovation where walls will be gutted near people on life support or people at risk of infection in the operating room, intensive care, or the neonatal unit. That hospital needs a construction manager who knows how to work without interfering with its services and the health of its fragile patients; we're the experts on that.

Enough clients are attracted by our expertise that we require no specified sales force and spend very little on advertising. We are a living example of "pull marketing," the concept in which reputation brings in business.

A Brief History of Elzinga & Volkers

1945: Peter Elzinga and John Volkers form a partnership to design and build homes in Fremont, Michigan. That and various projects in Holland, Michigan, lead to the incorporation of Elzinga & Volkers, Inc.

1950: Elzinga & Volkers grows regionally in western Michigan with major projects in various industries

1965: Ed Haltenhoff, the chief engineer of the state bridge authority—who oversaw the opening of the

Mackinaw Bridge connecting the Upper and Lower Peninsulas—joins E&V as general manager.

1977: After helping form GMB Architects and Engineers, E&V uses this partnership to establish itself as a national construction manager.

1985: Leadership of E&V is transferred to the company founder's sons, Marshall and Paul Elzinga, after Ed Haltenoff retires.

1988: Mike Novakoski joins E&V and the company, with operating offices in four states, is recognized as among the top one hundred US construction-management firms and a national builder of "big box" stores. E&V also has worked on more than 650 school projects around the country.

1994: Mike King joins the company as general manager and later becomes president and CEO.

1995: E&V Professional Services is established as a wholly owned subsidiary to serve the food and beverage industry with supplemental staffing and professional services.

2005: Mike Novakoski becomes president.

2007: E&V is first recognized among the 101 Best & Brightest Companies to Work For, which is the result of a new employee-centric corporate culture.

2010: Mike King retires as chairman and CEO, and company leadership transitions to Mike Novakoski and his executive team.

2015: E&V Professional Services is rebranded as the EV Group to reflect a new, broader service offering and growing client base.

2016: E&V is recognized as the Michigan Contractor of the Year for the second time, having first won the award in 2012.

To commemorate its seventieth anniversary in 2015, the company published a book titled *Unmistakably E&V*, which provides the full story of the many creative, dedicated, and talented people who built the firm. The book you're reading, in contrast, is organized around our ideas, not our company history. The first few chapters explain the genesis of our people-before-profits philosophy, how we came to realize it required right-brained leadership, and how we learned to lead from the heart. The next four chapters are about spreading the ideas outward from individual leaders into a company or organization's internal culture. We cover the processes of recruiting, onboarding and training employees, and the power of maintaining an employee-centric company culture. The final four chapters show what happens when the ideas are projected outward, so that you have an external culture that mirrors what happens within your walls and affects how clients, customers, partners, and the community regard you.

We struggled over the years to find a word or phrase to express our journey from competing on price in a commodity industry to becoming somewhat of an oddity in our industry (more about this in chapter 7). We tried out some taglines such as "the E&V Experience." Finally, the simplest term we found to express our vision was that we were *unmistakable* in every way.

We'll start at the beginning in chapter 1 with the origin of a new vision for our company.

CHAPTER 1

AN UNMISTAKABLE VISION: PEOPLE BEFORE PROFITS

We're going to recount how our company got onto the route toward a less bottom-line-oriented, more right-brained leadership. You may be surprised to learn it involved me getting an MBA with an emphasis in finance. So, how could that be?

—MIKE

Elzinga & Volkers was only my third job. I had a paper route from ages ten to sixteen, and I worked through college at a service station, pumping gas and fixing cars. Butch Paganelli, sole proprietor at Paganelli Shell, led his young staff with a lot of personality and heart. The stocky Italian-American made my time there fun and certainly memorable, even when he playfully threatened to put his size eight-and-a-half, triple-E shoe to my rear end if I didn't hustle out to the full-service island when a customer was there waiting.

After I got a degree in construction management from Ferris State University, E&V hired me right out of college in 1988. I started in a temporary position as an estimator and was promoted twice in project management in the first few years. You can see that, since I'm still at E&V, I have tremendous job loyalty. However, after a year or two at the company, I started to recognize I wanted to bring something different to the table. To set myself apart at a company owned by an architect and an engineer, I wanted to study business with an emphasis on finance. Getting an MBA was my way of bringing extra skills to the management team, and from what I read, a lot of company CEOs came from a finance background. I guess one could say that, at an early point in my career, I knew I needed to stand out and have a unique skill set to be considered unmistakably different! There were dozens of people like me competing for management's attention.

I was already starting to think about what I would do differently if I ran the company. One thing was obvious: those first two promotions resulted in no more pay. I went to my direct supervisor to ask why.

He said, "Well, jeez, look at what a great opportunity you have. You should just be appreciative of that in your young career." And I really understood the limitations of left-brained leadership for the first time. Probably, not much money would have been involved, but I felt slighted, and I questioned whether the company really cared about me. That was a turning point in my thinking about how a company should embrace its people and not treat them as just there to get the job done. I also didn't feel connected to anybody at E&V outside of my immediate project team. At a construction company, that can be as few as a half-dozen people.

A leadership transition began five years after I started with the company. The Elzinga family ownership's second generation was nearing retirement and decided to bring in a new CEO from the outside, Mike King, in 1994. He had a background in accounting and finance, and he had run a Fortune 500 construction company in California. He arrived with a bottom-line mindset, a focus on profit and loss statements. After a few years of night-school studies at nearby Grand Valley State University, I was the only one in the company at that time with an MBA. So, I had been trained in the idea that "maximizing shareholder value" was the primary goal of management. I could have used that knowledge to become Mike King's act-alike heir.

I knew that to grow as a leader I had to find mentors and become less introverted, so I got involved with various chamber of commerce leadership programs. I attended conventions where retired executives spoke, read a lot of business books, and finally came to a realization: what I yearned for was quite opposite of Mike King's left-brained approach. Left-brained business leaders watch the numbers, cut costs, seek the lowest price, and seldom seem to be enjoying their jobs. Their skills seem more like a burden than a gift. The right-brained approach is to lead from the heart.

> *I attended conventions where retired executives spoke, read a lot of business books, and finally came to a realization: what I yearned for was quite opposite of Mike King's left-brained approach.*

For a case study in one of my finance classes, I asked our CEO if he would share the company financials with me. He was more than happy to let me do my evaluations. Soon I was sitting in meetings with higher-up executives, offering ideas and different ways of attacking our business challenges. I was that cocky twenty-something who wanted to make things happen and was a little frustrated with the old school. When it came time for an annual review, one of the VPs said to me, "You're doing really well, but you need to make sure that you remain humble." And that was good advice, because I was in my mid-twenties and hadn't earned a place of respect yet.

So, from humble beginnings, a decade-long transition of our company began. I grew increasingly confident that Mike King's bottom-line decision-making, which ensured the company survived when it was financially much weaker, was not the way forward. Growth required hiring and retaining top talent—and making the company and its work *unmistakable.* We had not yet begun to use that word to brand our business approach, but it's the best label we've come up with for our concept of having happy, engaged, empowered employees who will do the right thing when nobody is watching. To fulfill those goals, we would have to put people before profits.

RIGHT-BRAINED PEOPLE SKILLS

Like a lot of industries, construction depends on people coming together as a team. We get a request for a proposal from an owner or architect, then we put in a proposal to build a project. We turn drawings on paper into reality. How profitable we are depends on the estimator getting the cost right, and the project managers lining up and overseeing all the necessary **trade contractors** that handle parts of the job. A field manager (commonly called a superintendent in our industry), a project engineer, and a field engineer all may be involved in coordinating the daily efforts with the support of the project manager and administrative staff back in the office. Each part of the job, such as concrete, steel, or carpentry, may have a foreman. In effect, the project manager and field manager are really people managers, coordinating multiple teams while also communicating with the owner and the architect.

What Is a Trade Contractor?

You'll notice this book avoids using the word "subcontractor." Years ago, we decided that the word was demeaning, and we began calling the skilled tradespeople we work with "trade contractors." As we began writing this book, we attended an annual awards ceremony for our local industry group in western Michigan and were delighted to find that it had not only adopted our terminology but was recognizing the general contractors and trade contractors on a more equal footing. (Chapter 8 has more details about this change in terminology.)

People skills—so-called "soft" skills—obviously come in handy with all that coordinating and communicating. Yet the construction industry is almost entirely male-dominated, and therefore led by more task-oriented, less expressive managers than some other industries.

A lot of things can go wrong in construction. Weather is beyond our control. Owners who hire us may not have been forthcoming about their price restrictions, schedule demands, or quality expectations. They may have hired an architect inexperienced with the specific type of project or who may be overwhelmed with work. Trade contractors may have felt pressure to bid a price for which they cannot meet our quality and safety expectations.

Imagine that a project is behind schedule, over budget, or the owner is unhappy about something. The general contractor's upper management must get involved and decide between callously enforcing the letter of the contract or doing the right thing to make sure that the client is pleased, and the trade contractors are treated fairly.

A left-brained leader like Mike King would be able to handle these decisions dispassionately. For example, he might anticipate that a risky situation needed to be priced higher for our protection. He might cut staff to control costs, something that kept our company alive through the Great Recession that began in late 2007. And if a client called thirteen months after project completion with a legitimate problem that would have fallen under a twelve-month warranty, Mike's default answer would be, "No, per our contract, we're not responsible to cover it," (although he didn't treat all situations that way). Mike's left-brained approach likely saved us a lot of irreversible pain during the recession.

As right-brained leaders, we've taken a long-term perspective on our relationships. We're not going to upset a client, possibly losing him or her for life, to avoid a small repair cost. We would take the same people-before-profits approach in building our team. Mike King would say, "You'll be lucky to keep people three to five years in this industry." For that reason, he didn't want to get overly invested in people, having seen nothing but high turnover. He didn't regard the workplace as the right place to make meaningful friendships, the kind that extend beyond work hours. At this late stage of his career, he was most comfortable managing from behind his desk, leaving it to others to handle the more social and community-service aspects of business leadership.

Much has changed within our company philosophy to encourage not only strong interpersonal relationships (sometimes even marriages) within our workplace as well as in the community.

Our vision was to have good people retire happy with the company, and we had to figure out how to get to that point. For us in Holland, Michigan, being involved in the city, with its business and religious institutions, helped us cultivate people skills and profitable relationships. If you are not familiar with Michigan, note that Holland is far from Detroit in many ways. It is a quaint town on the west coast of Michigan, the eastern side of Lake Michigan, about thirty

> *Our vision was to have good people retire happy with the company, and we had to figure out how to get to that point.*

miles southwest of Grand Rapids. The Dutch Reformed Church is the primary religious denomination. The main industry is heavy manufacturing, with office-furnishing companies such as Steelcase, Haworth, and Herman Miller in addition to automotive and battery plants. Ottawa county has the lowest unemployment rate in the state and some of the strongest philanthropy. The economic climate is very pro-business, with high ethics, and a lot of work done based on handshakes.

FAITH AND BRINGING YOUR BEST

Our clients around the country are always quite surprised when we set the bar beyond what any other general contractor has done for them. Now that we've reached the point where we are being recognized with awards for our unmistakable company culture, we can afford to tell you that the journey was not always smooth. It hasn't always been rainbows and unicorns. We had challenges getting the right players on the team, especially when we had rapid growth. We had to turn away jobs. We believe that if we don't have the talented people needed to flawlessly execute a job, we can't just say, "we'll figure out the resources later." We had some false starts in certain programs that we developed. We had the usual challenges too, such as illnesses and deaths, losing key customers, and economic downturns. You'll read in this book about how we kept the faith in our distinctive approach to business one day at a time by savoring successes, showing gratitude, and avoiding negativity.

We believe in living in the moment. We know that today is the thing that we can have the most impact on. We must not over-worry about tomorrow, but we can start to plan for a better tomorrow by asking, "How can we make it even better than anybody could have ever imagined?" We trust in a basic premise that has proven itself over time: "If we're going to bring the very best product, with the happiest, best employees, we're going to have more clients than ever, along with great success."

What we don't understand is why some competitors—even after they see our success—continue to do business the same old way. Maybe they lack faith in the idea that a people-centric business can be profitable. Maybe they are set in their ways, afraid of change, or uncomfortable with an approach that can seem touchy-feely to some people. It certainly was an adjustment for our seasoned construction-project leaders to learn to kick off their meetings with communication starters and team-building exercises. But the time and effort paid off. Putting a smile on the faces of ALL the people we touch is a joy. It has brought us energy, made work more fun, and has had a positive impact on the bottom line.

What we don't understand is why some competitors— even after they see our success— continue to do business the same old way.

The stereotypical construction worker is crude, unkempt, and poorly educated. Of course, we reject that stereotype, but we recognize that a macho culture permeates the industry, and it's admittedly hard to get the typical construction worker to discuss emotions—or even smile sometimes. When construction workers buy into what society tells them they should be, they reinforce the narrative. They don't shave, wear torn jeans, and generally appear intimidating. The business consequence is that some of the hospitals we work in won't let construction workers eat in the cafeteria or use their public bathrooms. This is why making workers happy, getting them to smile, is a step toward erasing a false narrative, and painting a different picture of our industry. We want them to know they can get ahead in our industry with right-brained traits such as being good communicators who are sympathetic to others' situations and willing to work together.

A LEFT-BRAINED LIABILITY

We know from experience that a general contractor who's a pain to work with not only loses customers but can even get charged more. At one time, we had an experienced and very technically competent project manager who was extremely left-brained. Derek, we'll call him, was all about making every single penny he could out of jobs. You might think our company would be happy to have a project manager skilled at finding the low bidder, but Derek would play games with them. He'd find loopholes to pay them even less, so he got a reputation. Trade contractors knew that if they were working with Derek, they needed to add a premium to the bid or they wouldn't make any money on the job. It didn't help that he cursed all the time and made up derisive nicknames for people, including his boss and the boss's wife. He would be the guy in the meeting who was looking at his watch, letting out deep sighs, and making annoying sounds by squeezing and tapping his plastic water bottle.

For most leaders, Derek would have been an asset worth putting up with because he was bringing in a lot of money. When our right-brained approach took hold, we saw him as a liability to our brand. When we let him go, we were thinking, "We owe it to our partners to provide people whom they can count on, who respect them, and who do their job in a very professional manner." Someone in Derek's position would oversee multiple teams. He would be the liaison between the field managers and the office, so people skills really were important. Although he was a technical wizard, he lacked the traits of a positive liaison and leader.

PERSPECTIVE ON LEADERSHIP

Not everyone is a natural at interpersonal relations. I came to realize that I needed to be the public face of our company as I moved up in leadership, and that would require some mentorship and study. I joined a local chamber of commerce leadership program of thirty people who meet once a month for nine months to learn about the community and to develop future chamber trustees. I did a few other similar programs to get a broader perspective on other people's leadership styles and to get out of my shell. Joining the Young Presidents' Organization in 2007 was instrumental. I get together with about sixty-five other western Michigan CEOs and, in smaller groups of six to eight YPO members called a "forum," I learned to share—at deep levels—the good, the bad, and the ugly of our businesses as well as our personal lives.

This network of peers provided perspective on leadership and helped develop the vision we are sharing in this book. At least four other E&V executives have attended various civic-leadership programs, reflecting our strong commitment to continually educate ourselves about the challenges that exist within our communities. More recently, business leaders in our city started a nonprofit training institute, New North Center, offering an Innovative Management Certification Program. We spent an eight-hour day there every Friday for thirty weeks, learning skills such as how to verbalize and visually communicate innovation. That rewarding program also informed this book, particularly the right-brained/left-brained concept. These training opportunities, and the broadening worldview that comes from serving on community and professional association boards, underlines the value of leaders seeking outside influences and perspectives. Desk-bound leaders who rarely immerse themselves in the world around them are typically out of touch and uninspired.

In this chapter we traced our route toward a less bottom-line-oriented, more right-brained leadership. It started oddly with the pursuit of an MBA and the realization that leadership requires humility, lifelong learning, and being open to new approaches—things generally not taught in MBA programs. In our case, we bucked the macho culture of the construction industry and invested in relationships, putting people before profits. The transformation of our company took place over a decade. The next chapter explains how we accomplished the shift in leadership style. You also will learn how visionary right-brained leaders in a corporate setting can benefit from having a certain type of collaborator.

Chapter One Toolbox

AM I RIGHT- OR LEFT-BRAINED?

By reading this book, you must have some desire to or curiosity in improving your corporate culture. While we can point to the many ways in which a positive, people-centric culture can improve your company's bottom line, some leaders may need motivation beyond dollars and cents. It is important to be honest about yourself as a leader. Ask yourself: Do I care about the people that work for me? Am I ready to do the hard work and treat people the way I would like to be treated? Do I have team members around me that will help carry the load? All of these questions are important to answer honestly before you set off on your journey.

This assessment is designed to help you understand if you naturally lean toward being right-brained, left-brained, or somewhere in-between.

Read each item carefully and decide how true each item is in describing you. Circle your response.	Never	Seldom	Occasionally	Often	Always
1 I enjoy diving into the details of how things work.	1	2	3	4	5
2 As a rule, adapting ideas to fit people's needs is easy for me.	1	2	3	4	5
3 Technical things fascinate me.	1	2	3	4	5
4 Being able to understand others is the most important part of my job.	1	2	3	4	5
5 One of my skills is being good at making things work.	1	2	3	4	5
6 My main goal is to have a climate that fosters supportive communication.	1	2	3	4	5
7 Following directions and filling out forms comes easily for me.	1	2	3	4	5
8 Understanding the social fabric of an organization is important.	1	2	3	4	5
9 I am good at completing the tasks I need to do.	1	2	3	4	5
10 Getting all parties to work together is a challenge that I enjoy.	1	2	3	4	5
11 I thrive on understanding the technical details of how my business operates.	1	2	3	4	5
12 I am concerned about how my decisions affect the lives of others.	1	2	3	4	5

Add your responses to the even-numbered questions. This is your right-brained score.

Next, add your responses to the odd-numbered questions. This is your left-brained score.

The higher of the two scores indicates whether your natural tendency is toward right-brain or left-brain thinking and how strong that tendency is on a scale from 0 to 30.

- If you are a left-brained manager, an engineer, or a number-oriented person, for example, our philosophy may be more of a challenge. But if you can be open to thinking about emotion-based people skills, you'll have the great opportunity to look at yourself differently and discover new strengths and powers. We know you like data and concrete results, so we'll offer you proof of concept.

- Those who enjoy building teams and continuously learning will greatly benefit from the concepts to come.

- The charismatic, humble, and giving servant/leader will have the easiest time with our approach. If that's you, maybe you don't need this book, but will find it provides you with validation and new ideas.

CHAPTER 2

PERFECT HIRES KNOW THEY'RE NOT PERFECT

At this point in our story, CEO Mike King, with his left-brained, accounting background, has started to appreciate having a company president who is wired a little differently and focuses on relationship building. Now the company needs to hire a vice president of operations. I contemplate the question, "What should that person be like?"

—MIKE

I interviewed more than a dozen candidates over three years for the position of vice president of operations, and never quite felt comfortable enough with any of them. I didn't know it at the time, but I was looking for somebody who was capable of leading from the heart *and* a master of the technical side of the construction industry. I wanted the unicorn that was artful at both building teams and building buildings. One day out of the blue I got a call from Tony

Roussey, the vice president of operations for a competitor, a family-owned business based about twenty miles away. The competitor was going through an ownership transition, and Tony didn't want to work for that family's next generation.

"I understand you guys might be looking," he said. "I've done some research. There are only three companies in West Michigan that I would even consider working for, and you're one of them. Is there any opening?" I said, "Yeah, as a matter of fact, let's chat." I had not met Tony and hadn't heard anything good, bad, or indifferent about him. But when he showed up to meet with Mike King and me for what we planned as a one-hour interview on a Friday, we ended up talking for three hours. That day, Tony and I both knew that E&V was the place for him. By Monday, Mike King and I had agreed on hiring Tony. Because Mike King was much closer to retirement, the decision hinged on my vetting someone who would best fit with my style.

Tony was on board within two weeks, and his hiring was instrumental to our cultural change. I didn't fully understand it at the time, but although we both had the same aspirations for the company, Tony would be the person able to implement the great ideas. I was more the dreamer, and Tony was the one who could integrate our vision into the business. A book published in 2015, *Rocket Fuel* by Gino Wickman and Marc C. Winter, helped us label the dynamic we saw at work in our leadership team. The authors of that business book described a *visionary* and an *integrator* as an essential combination to help a company thrive.

NEEDING A VISIONARY AND AN INTEGRATOR

Running a company without both a visionary and an integrator would be a challenge. We often tell a story about a very talented entrepreneur who started a business in his basement. He was full of big ideas and had a broad sense of the huge goals he wanted to accomplish. He grew a real business, but not at a rate that ever made him happy. He didn't have the ability to put his big-picture visions into bite-size pieces that could be acted upon. It took him more than ten years to find an integrator who helped him set up the systems and the processes and find the people and capital to properly execute his plan.

On the other hand, a company led by an integrator does really well at building and executing a business model. Over time, though, the business struggles to stay ahead of the market or the industry if its leadership is not creative enough to see new paths. A 1998 best-seller, *Who Moved My Cheese?* by Spencer Johnson, perfectly captured that risk of running a business with no visionary. A business can be great at doing the same thing over and over, and even getting better and more efficient, but then its product gets overshadowed or antiquated. It needs the dreamer in its leadership to change course or go to another level.

The leadership team that has formed at E&V is blessed with a nice balance of visionaries (myself and my co-author) and integrators (Tony Roussey and my brother, Joe Novakoski). That said, we do not mean to imply that these four co-owners of the business have strictly defined roles that only involve right-or left-brained thinking. Joe is an engineer who, very much like Tony, understands the relational side of the business. John grew up in the integrator world of technicians and builders, but is a visionary because he holds a place in his heart for big-picture and right-brained thinking.

In a job interview such as the one where I got to know Tony, it's not hard to vet an applicant's technical skills. As you might expect, Mike King asked Tony plenty of left-brained, production-oriented, systems-oriented questions. I probed for stories about his behavior and approach in certain challenging interpersonal circumstances. The stories Tony told about his experiences with other people really connected.

For example, in construction, the issue of safety is one where cost considerations constantly arise. I asked Tony in the interview about how we could afford to invest more money than our competitors did into making our job sites safer. He instinctively answered that nothing was more important than people's health and safety, and that putting the bottom line first was wrong. He said any job that results in an injury is a failure, regardless of how it meets goals for being on time, on budget, and of high quality. That answer just hit home for me, and I said, "This is the guy who gets it. He knows you can't run a business with profitability as the foremost focus. Profit will follow when you do the right thing in the first place."

Hungry, humble, and smart.

If you are a left-brained thinker, you're probably impatient for us to prove that concept, which we will do in the chapters ahead. On the way, we'll describe our goal of recruiting and retaining employees who are hungry, humble, and smart. Those three traits became the ingredients of our success before we really thought about how to best describe them. *The Ideal Team Player*, a 2016 business book by Patrick Lencioni, provided the terminology we now use to label the traits we came to value.

When we call someone "*hungry*," we mean they have drive and passion for what they do. They wake up thinking about how to do their job better. They constantly look for ways to benefit the company and to build better systems. Managers and coworkers who are humble and treat the people around them right attract other team players and together they bring success to an organization.

Humble people tend to give credit to others and shy away from the spotlight, no matter how much they deserve it. If they are also *smart*—the high emotional intelligence that is the third part of the trinity of characteristics we look for—they bring great success. In contrast, managers who have big egos tend to promote their own agenda, get by on an average (at best) effort, and often put their feet in their mouths.

We discussed how the visionary and the integrator bring different skills to the team, but that doesn't mean we throw out the importance of right-brained thinking for certain roles. Characteristics such as humility and being approachable make for better leaders and better team members. Being smart includes emotional intelligence, knowing how to respond to people and circumstances, knowing yourself and your strengths, and knowing how to handle relationships and social situations. For example, our CFO, Grace Silva, has those characteristics. Her job involves left-brained thinking. But her ability to understand and fit into our right-brained arena makes her an invaluable part of our leadership team.

A people-smart response to a situation can come from either the left or right brain. A right-brained thinker might have a more creative or compassionate response. A left-brained thinker might be able to quickly calculate the positive and negative implications of various ways of responding. In deciding to implement right-brained leadership in our company, we understood that we needed integrators with left-brained skills. But as you'll learn in the upcoming chapters, shaping our recruitment and personnel assessment around characteristics such as hungry, humble, and smart ensured we would have integrators who were able and willing to work under right-brained leadership.

Take, for example, our goal of having people who are hungry for more education and a better understanding of themselves. That goal requires building trust among employees from the day they come on board. We take time to run programs that allow us to dive deep into who we are and share that with our team so we're able to better understand the strengths and weaknesses of the people we work with, and so we can better rely upon each other.

We want our people to self-assess where they're at, attend retreats, accept mentoring, seek more training, and serve in community roles that promote their lifelong learning. A person who is humble, who knows he or she is not perfect, will fit into that kind of leadership orientation.

We use the Johari window—a traditional two-by-two matrix with four quadrants developed by psychologists Joseph Luft and Harrington Ingham—to promote people's enlightenment and understanding of who they are. The four quadrants represent:

1. what we and others know about ourselves

2. what others know about us that we are not aware of

3. what we know about ourselves that others are not aware of

4. what neither we nor others know about ourselves.

We push our people to not only be receptive to learning what others see in them, but also to get into that fourth quadrant and search for, discover, and own the truths hidden from themselves and others.

JOHARI WINDOW

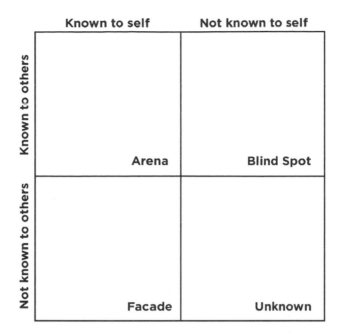

EVOLVING LEADERSHIP STYLE

Our transition as a company was a long journey. For the first few years, retirements and attrition necessitated by the Great Recession helped us eliminate some team members who lacked the character traits we needed going forward. Other changes happened more slowly. We read management books such as *Good to Great* by Jim C. Collins that inspired us, in light of the recession, to examine our business and focus on what we were best at and most passionate about. When the economy picked up, we set ambitious goals and started recruiting the right people, as we'll explain in chapter 4. Some luck or perhaps divine intervention must have helped us get perfect matches such as Tony. We have been blessed with extraordinary opportunities to make really smart hiring choices over the years.

> *Only after five or ten years did our clients, vendors, and trade contractors fully appreciate the value and permanence of our transformation. Our brand had attained what we half-seriously call our* **cult following***.*

When Mike King was still CEO, he scoffed that I—the other Mike—was Mr. Sunshine, an eternal optimist who thought we could fix anything with the right amount of time and attention. Now we've unapologetically imbued our leadership with optimism, and the sense that executives are responsible for owning problems. Kim Cameron, a University of Michigan professor and cofounder of the Center for Positive Organizational Scholarship, notes in his book, *Positive Leadership*, that "positive leaders are unusual in that they choose to emphasize the uplifting and flourishing side of organizational life, even in the face of difficulty."

At one point, we found that we had gone too far in painting a rosy picture. An anonymous survey revealed that our employees thought we were not being truthful enough and wanted us to share negative as well as positive information. We did that when we were showing losses from delayed projects in our first two quarters. Our team members appreciated our candor and without our prodding they overproduced in the next two quarters, allowing us to catch up before year's end. We didn't threaten to lay people off or cancel the holiday party, we just disclosed our earnings shortfall. Even as we presented some negative news, we made sure to move the discussion in a positive direction. The second part of the discussion focused on business-development prospects for the coming year. Bad things happen in business, but generally, we tend to focus more on the rainbows than the dark clouds. As author Kim Cameron suggests, organizations that strive for positive results should be conscious of maintaining a good ratio of positive news to negative news.

Mike Reflects on Positivity

My dad was a police officer. Money was tight with six kids, but our parents didn't burden us with their financial issues. If I needed a pair of shoes, my mom—the master financier in the house—figured out how to make it happen. I am grateful for my parents' sacrifices. They were upbeat. Their strong Christian values made them confident our family would be provided for no matter what, and we always were. They knew you didn't put parental stress on an eight-year-old child. So, I grew up as an optimist.

Having a fun and joyful workplace is important to our company culture. Here are two examples of how this plays out:

Investing in Some Fun

Warrior Dash, a crazy, dirty obstacle course-laden 5K, came to our area and put on its popular event on a Saturday morning. Competitors spend about forty-five minutes jumping over flames, crawling under barbed wire, and getting muddy. We offered to pay the $65 entry fee for employees and one guest who wanted to compete. A volunteer committee designed a cool "E&V Warrior" T-shirt with our company logo, which we paid for.

Some companies would balk at the cost of this endeavor, which was more than $6,000 to have around sixty people compete. But we found it an excellent investment, because the staff seemed totally changed the following Monday. We connected better, were re-energized, and more productive. If that event connected just two people together so they became closer friends at work and were happier and less likely to leave, the event paid for itself. How much does it cost to hire and train replacement employees, to get them up to speed? One key employee departure can easily cost a company $50,000 in lost productivity.

Mike Cherishes a Christmas Tradition

Taking time before Christmas to show appreciation with personalized, handwritten holiday letters is a favorite part of the job for me. I put my heart into the words I choose and wrap a gift box of items I select for the employee's family to open Christmas morning. Depending on the family's size and personal preferences, the box can contain cash, candy, varied gift cards, collectible coins, lottery tickets, or other items. The thank-you cards, smiles, and hugs tell me that employees know they are being treated with unusual warmth.

My reward is seeing how free people feel to come and share with me who they truly are, their hopes, their pains, and their joys. It just feels more real to know hundreds of family members have a better life because

> our employees love what they're doing, know why they're doing it, and realize we're all in this common front. When spouses come up and say, "My husband (or wife) has never been happier," that means a whole lot more than meeting some production goal.

For right-brained thinkers, getting confirmation that people are happier is equivalent to left-brained thinkers measuring an increase in productivity. We know happier employees have their hearts and minds actively engaged in their work. They look for ways to improve, tend to work harder, and keep clients more satisfied.

Along with our optimism, we work at maintaining intimacy, trust, and vulnerability among all of us in the company. The best way to explain this is with a story about our leadership team's first overnight retreat. We decided to go off-site to work on a three-year strategic plan. I told my assistant, Morgan, "I don't want people to stay overnight in a hotel where they all go back to their own rooms and are isolated there. I want to live, sleep, cook, and eat together for a three-day period."

Morgan, who has since been promoted to experience manager, an important job you will read about later in the book, had to find a big house we could rent for three days that would sleep more than fifteen people. Somehow, she found such a house just north of us and rented it sight unseen. We affectionately recall it as "the crack house" because it was dilapidated and in a terrible neighborhood. Those drawbacks were trivial compared to what happened there.

The top executives arrived first and discussed how we would run the retreat. Around five o'clock the field managers arrived for the night. We told them we would cook steaks together and have drinks around a backyard fire pit. But we also decided to take a risk and try some techniques learned from YPO to build intimacy and trust among a corporate team. We played an ice-breaker game called "two truths and a lie." You tell the group three things about yourself, of which only two are true, and everybody else has to guess which one is the lie. Around nine o'clock, we moved on to the next exercise. Everybody had been asked to bring one small but meaningful item of significance from their past to share with the group to help everyone get to know each other better.

By then we were sitting in a circle in the living room of "the crack house" with all the furniture pushed aside. Some of us had our mementos on our laps. The first person to speak opened a photo album and said, "This is an album of my daughter who I almost lost to a car accident when she was sixteen." We saw pictures of the car totaled, this girl on life support for days, maybe weeks in intensive care. The dad telling the story was a seasoned field manager in his late forties, strong enough that he could crush your hand with his handshake if he chose, but he was tearful. Everybody else was tearing up as he sent the album around. And that's how we learned that his daughter, our lovely young colleague Morgan, had that brush with death before we got to know her.

Then we went to the next guy, who reached into his pocket and pulled out a pebble. He said, "I remember a summer evening when my daughter was eight years old. I was sitting on my front porch, and I must have been looking really distressed. My daughter walked up to me—this young, sweet, little, innocent girl—and put her hand on my knee, bent down and reached into my landscape bed and picked up this rock. She opened my hand, placed it in my palm and said, 'Dad, I'm always here for you, if you ever need me, if you're ever worried, think of me and rub this rock.'" He said, "I've carried this rock in my pocket for the last eight years every day." Nobody knew that. There was not a dry eye after he shared that touching story.

The stories went on for two hours and they were all meaningful, but we'll end with one from a guy who showed us an International Harvester mesh baseball cap. He told us that when his dad, a widower, died, he got a call from somebody informing him that his brothers and sisters were already at dad's house taking all the stuff they wanted. Furious at that behavior, he got into his car, went over to his dad's house and confronted his siblings. On a hat rack, he saw the International Harvester cap his dad wore for thirty years. It reminded him of the tractor rides he got from his dad as a young boy. "This is all I need," he said, taking it and leaving.

By the end of the retreat, I remember that two of these rough, tough construction guys hugged each other and said, "I love you." They were grateful for the sharing and vulnerability that led to bonding like they had never experienced. We know if any of these construction superintendents gets a job offer or other opportunity to leave our company, there's no question that it will be like leaving their family. That term is used loosely in the business world, but these are people who have opened up to each other and feel safe together. That vulnerability is incredibly powerful, and we continue to hold retreats at all levels of our company.

In this chapter we discussed how right-brained leadership brings compassion, care, and love into a business to improve how people work together, as well as their happiness and productivity. We showed how having both a visionary and an integrator in this leadership is the best way to build a great business. We told you how we implemented right-brained leadership through our staffing and self-assessment, and deepened connections within our team. Now that you understand our leadership approach, you are probably wondering how to carry it out in the everyday business world. That's the subject of the next chapter.

Chapter Two Toolbox

Planning events and retreats is a common task for most business leaders. Taking time to focus on long-term planning, goals, and strategies is an ordinary and necessary part of the fiscal year. What may not be so common is using these retreats and planning sessions to form strong bonds within your team and create a level of trust and vulnerability that you can bring back to the workplace and begin using immediately.

Below is a list of suggestions on how to make your next retreat unmistakable. These activities and suggestions will help prepare your team for honest and open planning sessions and will improve the level of participation, input, and engagement during your events.

- Meet offsite.
  - Avoid the normal distractions of your office.
  - Consider a large vacation rental instead of a conference center or hotel.
  - Think couches over conference tables.
- Prepare a meal together.
  - Cooking together creates a situation where everybody depends on one another.
  - Cooking is a team-building exercise disguised as a necessary task ... everyone has to eat, right?

- Cooking together creates a setting for unstructured conversation, easing the group into the more serious, structured conversation to come.
- Create a shared, memorable experience.
  - Consider a physical activity or challenge.
  - Bring in a speaker or share a meaningful TED talk—teach the group something new that is indirectly connected to their work.
  - Consider completing a community service project together. For instance, have teams race to assemble a children's bicycle and then donate those bikes to a charity or a family in need.
- Get personal and connect at a human level.
  - Hold an activity where people are encouraged to share something important to them outside of the workplace.
  - Host an activity where your team is required to share a little bit about their past.
  - Customize the activity to the group ... smaller groups can share more where larger group may get less time.
- Leadership sets the level of vulnerability.
  - As the leader, you should go first in any activity to set the level of sharing through your response. Your team will follow your lead. When you take off your armor, others will be more likely to follow suit.

CHAPTER 3

LEADING FROM THE HEART

There have been several times throughout the course of our marriage that I have shared with my wife, Liz, that after her, our kids, and extended family, what really keeps me happy and excited about life is my job. I don't think much about retiring, but when I do it seems like a big step back from what has been a joyful part of my life. Building our company and developing relationships with the people in it and around it enriches my life. In a 2004 Harvard Business Review article titled "Success That Lasts," Laura Nash and Howard Stevenson identify four components of success: (1) happiness, (2) achievement, (3) significance, and (4) legacy. I believe what I am doing in my job today covers all four areas and gives me a feeling of true success. I feel sad for people who are counting down the weeks or years before they can retire or who are constantly checking their 401(k) as a ticket away from a miserable work life.

—MIKE

In the last chapter we mentioned feedback from our employees ranging from the formality of an anonymous survey to the informality of a smile and hug. But a simple question about retirement also gives us a measure of our success at leading from the heart. Suppose I approach one of our older employees and ask, "Hey, just curious, when do you think you'll hang up your hard hat and call it quits on this chapter in your life?" My goal is to get the answer, "I haven't really thought about it." There's an old saying: "If you love what you do, you'll never work a day in your life." Creating a workplace atmosphere that allows people to enjoy what they're doing makes the job more than just a means to an end. It hardly seems like a job if it becomes an important, rewarding part of their life.

Bosses who lead from the head and are always watching the numbers can't foster a caring and joyful workplace. We joke that some bosses lead from the "backside," taking the most pride in their ability to make tough decisions. We're focused in this chapter on how leading from the heart can be effective even in a business like ours where we always have to measure carefully. In construction, it's not a metaphor when we talk about following a blueprint, and that obviously requires some focus on numbers and (literally) concrete, hard-and-fast details.

For us, leading from the heart means inspiring the team

> *Leading from the heart means inspiring the team to execute a project in a way unlike any other. Our goal is not to maximize the profit from every job but to be pleasantly surprised with a better-than-expected bottom line.*

to execute a project in a way unlike any other. Our goal is not to maximize the profit from every job but to be pleasantly surprised with a better-than-expected bottom line. So, instead of every Monday morning looking at a cost report, we can judge success by the compliments we get from clients as they walk the jobsite with our field manager or email us afterward.

POSITIVITY AND LEADERSHIP STYLES

In any business, some bad news is inevitable. If we mess up and lose money on a project, we need to learn from the experience without taking it out on our people. If we have a bad quarter or lose a project we were counting on, we don't look outside the leadership team for someone to blame. Many if not most companies will look outside of the leadership team to figure out who fell down on the job. When leadership is looking for a throat to choke, "crap rolls downhill" becomes more than just an old saying.

The company's sales and revenue go up and down with the economy and other factors beyond our control. Spreading anxiety within the company about negative numbers takes employees' focus off the job in front of them. We try to keep that profit and loss information compartmentalized so negative numbers don't drag us down and affect how we treat our employees. The intent is not to cover up negative news, but to avoid burdening people unnecessarily. On the flip side, we go way out of our way to share positivity at all levels of the company to keep people happy and enthusiastic so they leave the office energized instead of drained.

People know from popular culture what heavy-handed leadership looks like. On *The Sopranos,* characters who didn't listen to the mob boss got whacked. In *The Devil Wears Prada*, the fashion-magazine editor played by Meryl Streep humiliates her personal assistant. Mr. Burns, the nuclear-power-plant owner on *The Simpsons*, always put profits before safety.

In real life, bosses don't have to be cartoonish villains to reject the idea of leading from the heart. Our former CEO, Mike King, believed people take advantage of executives who try to lead from the heart. He had cordial, friendly, respectful relationships with clients and employees. But he clearly came to work to make money, not to make friends. He believed that focusing on the numbers put business leaders in a better position when they needed to be the bad guy, to fire people, say no, or make demands. His background was in accounting and he focused on minimizing risk and making the numbers, not going out of his way to please people. Most of our employees didn't really know much about his family life, his hopes, pains, joys, and fears, because he didn't share that information like we do at our company today. We don't disrespect him for this; it's the culture he grew up in. He knew it to be right, in his mind, and in different times it worked.

When I served under him as president, I once gave an impassioned speech to a group in our boardroom. I don't remember what the emotional appeal was about, but I remember feeling good about getting a positive reception. I finished, sat down, and the other Mike stood up and said, "Now that Nova's done with his touchy-feely BS, let's keep going with the meeting." That putdown removed all the wind from my sails and became something of a company joke. But over time we embraced our roles as the touchy-feely guy and the numbers guy. I became the outward face of the company, with my office in sight of the reception counter, and the other Mike tended to stay in his office in the far corner of the second floor. That office arrangement was not overtly planned or discussed, but it said a lot about our leadership styles.

We still get some external pressure to conform to our industry's traditional leadership style. We did a joint venture with another construction company whose leaders made very clear that they don't believe in creating a deep relationship, for instance, between a field manager and a client's representative. Their rationale was that getting too personal would make it harder for them to remove people from projects when they wanted to. We shook our heads and quietly said to ourselves, "Good for you." Our experience was that the deeper the relationship, the more work the client gave us and the more they trusted us to make decisions such as replacing people.

VULNERABILITY AND REPUTATION

At one time, our company had a field manager whose technical knowledge was lagging but who had a masterful way of dealing with people. He was humorous and joyful, and brought excitement to his work. His jobs went better than those managed by our more technically skilled field managers. I saw how he and some other people I worked with displayed vulnerability and yet drew respect by being themselves. People loved and trusted them even more when they saw that they were less than perfect. I was always drawn to that type of leader, and decided to become one myself, putting my imperfections out there and becoming more approachable.

If you build a better workplace, people want to join it. In 2010 we hired someone who had left a competitor and later promoted him into leader-

> *If you build a better workplace, people want to join it.*

ship. He stays in touch with past coworkers from his prior employer, telling them about some cool things we do. A few years later, one of those former coworkers approached us for a job and was hired. Six months later another did the same. We had three excellent, experienced field managers talking about how great our company is and lamenting how long they stayed at their old job. Soon a fourth one jumped ship, and the owner of the competitor company called and said, "Mike, you're killing me. You've got to stop doing this."

We ended up having a long conversation to explain how we were not poaching people; they just were not happy where they were. They came knocking on our door, and we should not feel bad about that. They left a place where they were managed by the book, without compassion, to come to a workplace where their happiness was a priority. One story I was able to share with the owner involved his field manager asking to leave work a bit early to go to the dentist and getting docked for a half-day of vacation. This was someone in a salaried position who worked sixty hours a week, often far from home, and had recently stayed on an out-of-state job through a holiday weekend.

We still get applicants from that competitor, so apparently that company can't get beyond its left-brained fixation on following black-and-white rules. In fact, a member of the competitor's leadership team joined us after growing tired of being criticized for bringing up the emotional side of business decisions. A right-brained leader will know enough about the organization and its people to realize when employees are owed more than what's spelled out in the manual of standard operating procedures. The purpose of such a manual, of course, is to avoid labor-law complaints, getting sued for discrimination, and so on. But those risks are minimized when a company has responsible leaders who are committed to solving people's individual problems: when it has no disgruntled employees! No manual can cover every situation, so the rules should not be applied rigidly to every situation. People need to be involved in solving people problems.

CARING AND HAPPINESS

We were not attracting our competitor's veteran field managers with more prestige or perks. In fact, one of them had just completed a multimillion-dollar, 350,000-square-foot building for the competitor. We put him on a less prestigious $2 million job, a 20,000-square-foot building. He had been driving a brand new, decked-out, 4x4 extended-cab truck, we gave him a workhorse of a truck. I met his wife at a breakfast and she told me he had never been happier in his life—because he was now part of a team that cared about each other.

We also hire people with two or three years' experience away from major construction companies that recruited them out of college with the promise of glamour. In our business, glamour is building a skyscraper or working on a $200 million construction site. Instead we offer individual growth-training plans and relief from being treated like a replaceable part in a huge corporation. That's not to say that giant companies don't have the same opportunity to think creatively about people. Too often they just use their size and complexity as an excuse to manage by the book and not care about their people individually.

Leading from the heart begins with rejecting the idea that responsibility for an employee ends with signing the paycheck. Many employees sign on for a job that involves substantial sacrifice—long hours, being on-call, checking email late at night and on weekends. Furthermore, at F&V we ask our employees to be extraordinary to our clients, to think creatively, and to help make our company unmistakable. For that, we owe them more than just a paycheck.

If you are a left-brained boss, you may be thinking to yourself that you have provided employees a big, expensive thing besides their paycheck—health insurance. But after the Affordable Care Act was signed into law in 2010 by President Obama, there was a growing trend to shift the cost burden away from employers. Our health-insurance consultant pointed out that the law didn't require us to provide health insurance for an employee's spouse who worked for another company that offered insurance. Why should that other company escape the cost while we cover the whole family? We exercised our right to send spouses to their own employers for insurance, and quickly heard from employees urging us to reconsider. In respectful, well-thought-out letters, they said it would be a financial hardship for a couple to have two plans each with a high deductible requirement, almost $5,000 total out of pocket.

The left-brained, P&L-driven leader would have simply said, "Not my problem." We, on the other hand, did not want to put a financial hardship on a group of employees. We rescinded the policy for existing employees at a cost of about $20,000 per year, and decided to take this issue into consideration in the compensation of future employees. We got applause at the announcement. A woman with small children who was affected because they were being insured through our company, not her husband's employer, came up to me, Mike, with a big hug and said, "We were praying to the good Lord about how we were going to make this work financially."

Spending money to save money for a spouse's employer is the downside. The upside is we showed our employees we were willing to listen to them. They didn't just grumble among themselves, but felt they could approach us with an issue, which was a proof of concept for our years of right-brained management. We had made a left-brained policy decision without toggling back to the right brain to check on the effect on our employees—a lesson for us in making future decisions on benefits. We can't avoid asking our employees to pay more for their health care to keep up with inflation, of course, but we have learned to analyze all aspects of such a change.

One of the most common examples we see in the business world of left-brained shortsightedness is when executives respond to downturns by dropping the company picnic or Christmas party. You totally disconnect from the spouses you maybe see once a year, thereby losing a chance to gain their support and appreciation for the company. The small savings are not worth the loss of goodwill. The same goes for cutting back free office lunches or 401(k) matches in a recession or down year, when, typically, you are also asking employees to work harder and maybe forgo raises.

A company with a $5 million overhead is pinching pennies, not being financially prudent, if it cancels a $10,000 Christmas party. The cancellation impacts all employees and their spouses, so the savings per person is negligible.

Business leaders should be able to think of a way to save $10,000 with more limited impact on people. Business owners, who get most of the gain in good times (rightfully, because they are taking on the capital risk), should also be ready to take on a proportionate amount of pain in difficult times. To put it all back on the people who make you the money seems out of whack. A right-brained leader can instinctively calculate the return on investment of things like holiday parties that show up only as costs on the balance sheet. We just know we are doing the right thing, that people will be happier, and happier people will make happier customers—and make us a more successful company.

Any of our people, from carpenters to senior leaders, can cost the company $10,000 instantly with a bad on-the-job decision. When employees decide how to pour a concrete slab or put together a steel fabrication, think how much a do-over would cost. A more productive, engaged workforce that is looking out for each other's safety and the company's best interests can easily save $10,000 many times over in the course of a year.

EXAMPLES OF LEADING FROM THE HEART

Here are some more examples of leading from the heart with right-brained thinking:

- As our company grew more sophisticated, some of our longtime employees were no longer able to do the job as well as before. We told them, "Listen, it's not going to work. But we want you to leave with your head held high. We want you to be proud of the time that you served." We extended the separation process and helped place some of them in new positions with clients. When they were ready to leave, they could announce they had given two weeks' notice. There was no layoff-related impact on morale. They didn't miss a paycheck, and we got some value from their service during a time they might otherwise have collected unemployment compensation.

- We had a very talented project manager who weighed in the neighborhood of four hundred pounds. At his annual review, his weight was, pardon the pun, the elephant in the room. Nobody wanted to talk about it. HR consultants might be horrified by this story, but as we were wrapping up his annual review, I told him how worried I was about his weight. "I want for you to walk your beautiful young daughter down the aisle someday. I am so worried that I will come in on a Monday and hear you died of a heart attack. Is there anything I or the company can do for you?" So began a pretty incredible journey for him that resulted in surgery and significant weight loss. We hired a personal trainer and paid his gym membership because we cared about him. It changed his life. His wife ended up losing a lot of weight, too. His whole family dynamic changed. He's kept that weight off and is much more successful today. He started his own business, with our support and coaching. He has often said, publicly, that my frank discussion with him was just what he needed to make the changes he always wanted to make. He truly appreciated the sincerity of our caring approach and the heartfelt reasons for putting our fears into words that motivated him.

- One of our competitors, a company we respect greatly, lost a life on a job. We sent flowers and a sympathy card to their office. We received a letter back from them saying none of their other competitors had done so, and they were touched. Our view was that we collectively lost a life in our industry, they were going through a horrible thing, and it could have happened to us.

In our everyday business life, leading from the heart most often involves making decisions that require balancing our SOPs against concerns that following a policy strictly would not be the right thing to do. We have to toggle back into that right brain and ask, "How would I feel if I were in this person's shoes?" Most of the time, we err in favor of the employees. That means treating policies more like guidelines. This may sound unwise or possibly even discriminatory, but usually these are not situations that could get us into trouble. They are more like the example above of letting someone leave early to go to the dentist.

We know that just because a rule is in writing doesn't mean it always wise to follow. We get construction drawings that call for us to put in a wall in a way we know is not sound. We don't just follow the drawings and let the wall collapse! Most contractors will challenge any physical plan they think will fail. Unfortunately, when it comes to a conflict between the bottom line and the best interests of their people, we've seen in this chapter how business leaders sometimes fail to lead from the heart. Some may consider it too touchy-feely or fear being taken advantage of. When there are business setbacks, financial challenges, or hard decisions, it's easy for leaders to shift blame or burden to their people. But, ultimately, it's smarter and more successful to engage right-brained thinking. Once business leaders have learned to do so, the next step is to spread the approach through their company or organization. The next chapter addresses how to recruit and build a team that's open to becoming unmistakable.

Chapter Three Toolbox

BE AWARE OF THE TOGGLE.
KNOW WHEN TO SWITCH IT.

LEFT BRAIN

Analytical
Mathematical
Pragmatic
Scientific
Black & White
Sequential
Practical
Detailed

RIGHT BRAIN

Intuitive
Emotional
Visceral
Cognitive
Creative
Spatial
Approximate
Artistic

CHAPTER 4

IMAGINE CREATING A SELF-REGENERATING TEAM

I toured a company that was under consideration for furnishing one of our projects. The company had cultivated a reputation for providing fun workspaces for its employees as a perk to help it attract creative, high-end designers. As I passed through the areas where they had the ping-pong and foosball tables and beanbag chairs, I noticed the lights were off. I commented about how the fun spaces were deserted, and the person giving the tour said, "You don't want to be the one caught playing foosball right now." A recession had hit the furniture industry hard and led to cutbacks. Left-brained worries about productivity had overtaken the supposed fun culture when it was most needed. My right-brained thinking was that a true company culture should not be disposable in a bad economy.

– JOHN

Do you work in an industry where labor supply and demand stay in perfect balance? Do future leaders line up at your door begging for admission, always embrace your company culture when hired, and remain loyal employees until retirement? More likely, if you are a business leader, you know the frustration of dealing with labor shortages and the cost of high turnover, two challenges we regularly face in the construction industry. We recruit workers for laborious jobs where they'll get sweaty, climb into trenches, and usually leave work dirty. To make matters worse, those in construction are stereotyped in popular culture as unshaven, wolf-whistling bruisers who carry a metal lunch box to work and head to the bar afterward to drink beer all night. Under the surface of this stereotype is an assumption that the labor is backbreaking, and the workers are unprofessional and uncaring with a TGIF, just-a-job attitude.

> *The competition for skilled labor is a survival-of-the-fittest situation in which companies need to be fit in not only their balance sheets but also culturally. That's where leading from the heart, treating our people really well, gives us an advantage.*

We employ workers from many trades—carpenters, steelworkers, and concrete workers to name a few—who have lots of choices of where to go. Skilled trades have **high demand and short supply**, an issue that also affects manufacturing industries. The trades-worker shortage began when the 2007–2009 recession forced skilled workers into other industries, and they did not return when the economy recovered. The number of people entering the trades is not keeping up with the demand and the retirement rate. The competition for skilled labor is a survival-of-the-fittest situation in which companies need to be fit in not only their balance sheets but also culturally. That's where leading from the heart, treating our people really well, gives us an advantage. The backdrop for everything we're doing to try to attract and retain the best people is that our company's survival is at stake.

Our Supply and Demand Problem

Demand for commercial construction has been high across the United States. As we're writing this book, 93 percent of contractors are expecting to see equal or greater profit margins in the next year, according to the Commercial Construction Index. The index, produced by the USG Corporation and the US Chamber of Commerce, surveys contractors each quarter to gauge sentiment and measure the health of the construction sector. Despite demand, 95 percent of contractors reported difficulty finding workers for their projects because of an ongoing skilled labor shortage.[1]

For twenty years we've fought to be brought in at the beginning of construction jobs as equal members of a team that includes the architect and the building or project owner. So, our people dress professionally, reflecting their higher education and use of expensive technology. Creating a sense of pride in what they do lays the ground-

---

1   USG Corporation, and US Chamber of Commerce, *USG + U.S. Chamber of Commerce Commercial Construction Index: 2018 Q1*, March 6, 2018..

work for performing their jobs in a professional and caring way that pays off by pleasantly surprising customers.

COMPETING FOR TALENT

Our area of western Michigan has so much heavy manufacturing that there is unhealthy competition for labor. We hear about this when we build plants designed specifically to attract skilled workers to jump ship from a competitor. We're happy to have this work, but the idea behind it is shortsighted.

Suppose you have a metal stamping plant that gets really hot inside by midsummer. A new competitor comes to town saying, "I'm going to have an air-conditioned plant." The idea is that even without higher pay, employees will jump from their miserable hot plant to join the new company. Making employees more physically comfortable in the summertime falls short of what we mean by treating your people right. If management treats them well, and they have a comfortable emotional environment year-round, they'll be smiling even when it's hot. In Michigan, it's only hot for three months, so what happens come September? Year-round happiness is a more important goal.

Retention is an issue in all kinds of workplaces. Since we have shared our approach with our local chamber of commerce, that office has created great retention. The reality for nonprofit organizations is that people don't work there for the money. They will jump around in the sector if they are not happy. With tight budgets and little flexibility to offer raises, nonprofits have to treat their

> *With tight budgets and little flexibility to offer raises, nonprofits have to treat their people well.*

people well. Our local chamber invested in a new, modern workspace that facilitates teamwork. The leadership holds annual overnight retreats and works on creating relationships among the staff—not based on titles and hierarchy but on peers coming together arm-in-arm to execute the mission of the chamber for its members.

People have many different jobs in the chamber office: marketing to attract new members; event planning; financial consulting to help businesses find capital and grow; data collection and surveys; general administration. If each person hired came into his or her own little silo, the organization would lose its dynamic. Another nonprofit could cherry-pick employees who felt no connection to the organization beyond the paycheck and immediate job responsibilities. So, the smart nonprofits have figured out how to create a workplace environment that is highly desirable, where people feel like they are working with their best friends and have an emotional attachment to the spirit of the workplace.

Long-term holistic solutions to employee retention and recruitment don't involve artificial lures such as ping-pong tables that workers are afraid to use. Real lures are harder to come by because management can't just write a check. Creating a lasting positive culture takes constant work, genuinely caring about people, understanding who they are, and helping them develop.

Different lines of work face different challenges in recruitment and retention. In construction, we encounter people with low expectations thinking, "Billy's not smart enough to go to college. Let's go have him wrench plumbing pipe." Since we're looking for smart people, we push back and tell parents that entering the skilled trades can be a smart decision. A college degree won't necessarily earn someone more money. One of our company's vice presidents, whose son is a public-school administrator, hears about teachers making only $36,000 annually when they're six years out of college and carrying $60,000 in student loan debt. We tell parents about the carpenter who's making $63,000 after eight years in our business, has no debt, will get more raises, and enjoys great job satisfaction. His work is different all the time, and he can drive by and see his accomplishments even many years later.

In most trades, high school graduates can apprentice and become skilled journeymen in four to five years and be earning great money by their early twenties. A journeyman electrician could then decide to go back to college for an electrical engineering degree, for example, possibly even with an employer helping to pay tuition. The push in recent decades to get more students a college education has led to enormous loan debt and made recruitment more difficult not only in construction but also in manufacturing. Readers interested in learning more about efforts to encourage young people to get trained for skilled jobs can look up the MikeRoweWORKS Foundation, led by the host of the Discovery Channel television show *Dirty Jobs*.

Mike Reflects on Shop Class

I went through a vocational program in residential construction during my junior and senior years of high school. An instructor named Howard Huyser said, "Hey, you've got a real knack for leadership." He pointed me toward a university program in construction management, because he had come to understand how much I loved construction but didn't want to be working a shovel when I was fifty. Kids who have a dad who is a policeman or a plumber, may naturally gravitate toward those careers because it's what they see. Others need to be exposed to work such as construction and the trades taught in shop class to see if they like doing it.

Not every job is exciting but even the hardest work can be made attractive by business leaders treating their people with dignity. Imagine being a construction worker and being told to eat lunch in the dusty corner of a building under construction. Then go use a poorly maintained portable toilet that has been baking in the sun or is freezing cold. We understand that clients are concerned our construction workers might track dirt into their buildings. But we give our

> *Not every job is exciting but even the hardest work can be made attractive by business leaders treating their people with dignity.*

people enough uniforms so that they can come to work each day in a clean, dignified uniform; they are not going to go into somebody's company cafeteria in a ratty beer T-shirt. If we are working in a sensitive environment such as a medical center that won't let our tradespeople use the facilities, we provide a clean, heated or air-conditioned trailer for their breaks. It might cost an additional $300 a month to give fifty workers respect. A smart contractor will pass the cost on to the building owner.

RESPECTING FRONTLINE LEADERS

Another inexpensive and easy way to give laborers dignity is to offer them opportunities to be organizational leaders. We might ask them to talk in a one-minute video about some innovation they brought to their jobs. The videos are available companywide and shown at meetings, where each innovator is applauded for making an improvement and being an organizational leader. That's something a concrete worker can talk about at home or with buddies, helping us with recruiting and retention. Not only does sharing their ideas give the workers a sense of pride, it keeps our workplace innovative and inspires productivity, which any business can appreciate.

Calling a frontline worker a leader reflects the reality of our company having inverted our organizational chart. The CEO's main job is to support the four executives who directly report to him, so they are in effect above him on the chart. When you get to the top of the chart, where the CEO traditionally sits, that's where we put our trade workers. They are the ones who interact with our customers every day and provide value, so we recognize them as leaders. We empower them to lead corporate change, though maybe even in small ways.

ORGANIZED WITH AN INVERTED ORGANIZATION CHART

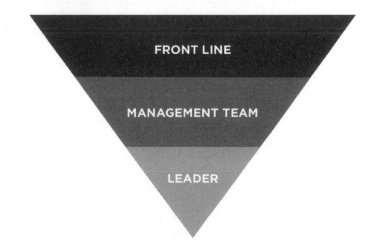

Too many executives see workers as just tools to get a job done. When an executive thinks of laborers as human beings, respects them, gets to know them outside work, and learns their spouses' names, workers want to stay at that job. Changing the workers' attitude so they don't think of themselves as at the low end of society promotes pride in their work. That pride improves quality and creates value for the company that customers can see.

By contrast, employees who have bad attitudes toward work are toxic, especially at a company following our right-brained approach. We are referring to people who say hurtful things, act disengaged at meetings, and always look like they think they have something better to do. These people can't be organizational leaders, though they sometimes think of themselves as highly valuable and untouchable. One cocky salesman whom we let go years ago felt sure our company couldn't survive without him.

"We could have been something together," he said while shaking hands on his way out. Now our company has tripled in size and he would have had a tough time finding a better job than that growth afforded. Similarly, a departing manager in one of our divisions said, "This company will fail without me." She had not embraced our cultural change, didn't understand it, and we had to let her go. We want employees who are hungry, humble, and smart, not ones who think they are the center of the universe.

In cleaning house to get rid of toxic influences, we also consider the destructiveness of gossip. We had a longtime administrator who was not very

> *We want employees who are hungry, humble, and smart, not ones who think they are the center of the universe.*

productive and was also only a few years from retirement. Keeping this employee would have been an acceptable legacy cost, but we realized her vocal negativity and spreading of gossip was having subtle impacts on others. We asked her to keep her opinions to herself, but she persisted in figuratively contaminating the company water cooler. Eventually, we let her go—after providing multiple warnings and carefully documenting the reasons.

GROWING OUR OWN TALENT

As we recruit replacements for company veterans, it is tempting to look for someone with ten, twenty, or even thirty years of experience rather than invest time and energy in training somebody new to the industry. That's the easy way out, though it's riskier than some business leaders realize. Experienced people come with their own belief systems. We tell them our business philosophy and they nod their heads, but we sense they're thinking, "I hear you but I'm going to do it my way." Not long ago, Tony Roussey, who has since become our chief operating officer, actually heard those words from one of our newly hired field managers, a thirty-year veteran in the industry. This defiant attitude was a red flag that ultimately led to us parting ways with someone who had all the technical skills needed to do the job. Holding true to your cultural beliefs may cost you some technically capable people, but individuals who resist the organization's culture will ultimately do more harm than good.

We have had success identifying young talent early and mentoring them to become the leaders we want them to be. When replacing a middle manager with ten years of experience, we may opt to take someone with only five years of experience. Our approach requires extra effort in recruiting and training, which we will discuss in the pages ahead, but it pays off when measured from a right-brained perspective.

In the recruitment process, we must dig a little deeper, interviewing candidates not only for technical ability but also for personality and cultural fit. In making the hiring decision, that "hungry, humble, and smart" personality who fits our company culture may outweigh factors a left-brained manager would use to measure ability, such as technical certifications, education, and grade-point average. We are asking ourselves, "Would I like to spend time with this person after work?" We are asking, "Can I see myself working with this person?" rather than just assessing whether the candidate can do the job. Many of our competitors have tried to get to know candidates by administering personality or behavioral assessments. Standardized, multiple-choice tests have some value, but not for measuring cultural fit, which we believe is something you need to *feel* to understand.

Hiring someone just out of high school or college obviously means we are not going to get the same level of talent and experience. But most of our current leadership team came in that way, which is one reason we have our unique, home grown company culture. We are looking for people we can mold into the type of leaders we need. We look for job candidates willing in an interview to admit their mistakes and discuss not only their abilities but also their vulnerabilities. We might ask, "Tell me a time you made a bad decision, and how did you make amends or how did you rectify it?" Applicants who can discuss

> *We look for job candidates willing in an interview to admit their mistakes and discuss not only their abilities but also their vulnerabilities.*

learning a lesson the hard way show they know themselves and are humble about their imperfections. Job candidates must highlight their successes, but the ones who impress us do it without bragging. They also tend to credit others with comments such as, "I was part of a team. It wasn't just me."

ASKING HOW WE ARE DOING

The job candidates we are looking for are also willing to accept criticism. Our company culture requires being open to outside perspectives. We work with a lot of trade contractors, and we ask them how our people are doing. That's more unusual than you might think if you are not in our rough-and-tumble construction industry. An electrician who thinks he could be making more money on a job, for example, can be very opinionated about a general contractor's managers or even the accounting staff. But we want 360-degree feedback, meaning we ask everyone around us for an honest appraisal of our job performance. That feedback, which can be delivered through an HR consultant, makes some people very uncomfortable. But employees who want to get better at their jobs are willing to ask, "What do people know about me that I can't see?" They will take the answers to heart and work on improving. (In chapter 2 we discussed the psychological technique called the Johari window that supports this approach.)

What Mike Says About Criticism

Even though I don't report to anyone, all our people are judging me. Do I have the ability as a leader to accept their criticism, constructive or otherwise, and own some or all of that? I have to—because more than likely, they're right. If three people say I'm not handling a situation well, I'm probably not.

The great thing about outside perspective is that it can be positive and a basis for improvement and growth. Part of our effort to get outside appraisals of our company involves entering contests where we have won awards based on independent surveys of our employees, trade partners, and customers. We'll discuss the usefulness of those awards further in chapter 9, but our point here is that the process includes honest feedback that helps us improve.

We believe that any of our employees may have good ideas we need to hear. We have talented people who could very well be vice presidents if the positions opened. But they don't need the job title to be heard, because we have found a way to say, "We want to use your knowledge." We created two groups, the Office Leadership Team and the Field Leadership Team for the talented frontline people who might not have an immediate advancement opportunity but are highly regarded as leaders. Appointing them to the leadership teams not only bestows an honor but allows them to help lead organizational change because, unlike their CEO, they are close enough to the ground to see problems and carry out creative solutions.

The advantages of this program begin with recruitment. When a job candidate asks, "What is my ability to advance?" we can honestly say even a carpenter with five years' experience can be in an executive-level position in our company. That's true because any employee with enough organizational leadership ability can be on one of our leadership teams. We have people in their twenties on these teams attending annual retreats with the executive committee. Together, about fifteen of us look at goals for the next quarter and the next year, and how we're going to build and execute our business plan.

The leadership teams are assigned tasks and responsibilities. They are empowered to act in a corporate leadership role as they meet throughout the year and develop programs.

In chapter 2 we discussed how companies need visionaries and integrators. The two leadership groups are integrators as they handle the rollout plans for ideas the top executives would never have had time to implement. (We give an example when we discuss the Blueprint for Success Program in the next chapter.) Being on the team is an honor that allows those people to shine in front of their peers at a company-wide annual meeting. It's also rewarded with bonuses specific to their roles.

NOT WAITING FOR VACANCIES

For our left-brained readers who are eager for proof that the ideas we have been discussing have tangible bottom-line benefits, there's this: At Elzinga & Volkers, the turnover of employees who feel they can do better elsewhere is less than 1 percent in a low-unemployment economy, which saves us time and money on recruiting and training. At the same time, we are growing and need to maintain a bench of prospective employees we can bring on when we have openings. Experienced people are knocking on our doors because they have heard about our culture and are not satisfied with their current jobs.

This demand from potential employees has created a unique situation for us. We are constantly interviewing potential candidates even if we don't have an opening. If we find a good fit, we make an offer. We agree on the compensation and benefits, they shake on it, but rather than increase overhead when we don't need it, these pre-arranged, future employees go into our "Virtual Employee Waiting Room." This way, our competitor pays our future employees while they're waiting for us to call them. We've had senior project managers happily wait six months for our call, because they knew they had lined up the future job they wanted.

Does your culture attract talent before it's needed?

This Virtual Employee Waiting Room may have a dozen people in it at any given time. If we land a big contract and need to bring on a highly qualified manager quickly, we can do so in only two weeks. A company whose culture doesn't allow for such a waiting room has worse options for filling such a gap: Acting hastily, settling for the first applicant who comes along, overlooking a candidate's liabilities, and making a poor short-term decision that can have a negative long-term impact. Alternatively, they may pay more to poach a competitor's talent, or put up with a vacancy while they begin sifting through piles of résumés. Each of those options carries risks and can detract from success.

We have discussed various aspects of our recruiting and team-building process, but the common element was knowing what our company really stands for. We are a for-profit business, so people we meet reasonably assume we exist to make money. If you asked us, we would give a different answer: "We think E & V exists to put a smile on the face of everyone we touch." As business-leadership expert and author, Simon Sinek maintains, it's very powerful to have a "why-we-exist" that is understood by all.

We think any organization in any industry could use the motto: "Do your job like no other to create smiles on the faces of others." When the motivation for working hard is a bonus, and it makes you smile on the one day a year it arrives, the job becomes all about making money. After you use the bonus to pay a few bills, you spend the rest of the year making the owners money so they can pay for their boat. Employees recognize and are affected by the difference between owners who are out for themselves and those who display humility and vulnerability. If the motivation is

> *Do your job like no other to create smiles on the faces of others.*

putting a smile on the faces of all the people you work with and meet, your enthusiasm will make your clients or customers happier. You will make more money, use it to create more smiles on more faces year-round, and it just builds.

Maybe because we are in an industry where recruiting and retaining talented people is difficult, we had to use our right-brained ingenuity to make our workplace more fulfilling. You've seen in this chapter how we found success by treating people right: recruiting hungry, humble, and smart employees; weeding out those with toxic attitudes; and breaking up responsibility for leadership beyond traditional roles. The company culture has become a magnet for talent, helping us carry out our "Smile vs. $" approach. The next chapter will dig deeper into how processes within an organization connect with business success.

Chapter Four Toolbox

FORMATION OF A LEADERSHIP TEAM

In this chapter, we explored the power of having a leadership team comprised of team members who are embedded in your operations, not just your executives. This team will help you disseminate information through the organization and aggregate ideas and issues up to the executive team. They will become trusted resources and help carry the load of cultural and operational initiatives. Because their value is so high, picking the right individuals is critical. Here are some tips on organizing your team:

1. Limit the team to ten to fifteen people, including your executive staff. This number is ideal for creating strong connections through trust and vulnerability, which leads to honest sharing of feedback and ideas. This is also a great number for planning retreats and visioning exercises.

2. The leadership team should be a representative cross section of your organization. For us, that means that we have representation from our field operations and our office operations. Avoid selecting your department leaders just because of title. Remember that this group is meant to be visionary and strategic, not just operational.

3. Look for the influencers in your organization, the people that, when they buy into an idea, others

around them follow suit. These will be the people that will create buy-in quickly in your organization.

4. Look for high performers with high potential rather than tenured employees. That is not to say that these leaders are not your more senior employees, but make sure they fit the other necessary criteria of an organizational leader. The matrix below can help you identify potential candidates. Focus on employees who fall into the upper right-hand boxes. These are the employees that will get the most out of their involvement on the leadership team will give you the best results.

ROLE/POSITION TITLE

POTENTIAL		LOW	MED	HIGH
	HIGH	**Enigma** Wrong job Wrong manager Needs intervention	**Growth Employee** Challenge, reward recognize, develop	**Future Leader** Reward, recognize, promote, develop
	MED	**Dilemma** Provide performance coaching challenge to enhance performance	**Core Associate** Motivate, engage and reward	**High-Impact Performer** Challenge, reward, grow, motivate
	LOW	**Under Performer** Move up or out	**Effective Associate** Engage, focus, motivate	**Trusted Professional** Retain, reward, coach to develop Others

PERFORMANCE

CHAPTER 5

YES, WE WANT YOU TO DRAW US A PICTURE

In the civil-engineering world, a sieve is a device made up of a series of screens to dump gravel through, sorting it from big to small particles. Sieve analysis tells us what material we are working with. We're not the first in our industry to use the screening metaphor in personnel assessment. But we've built a Sieve Analysis/Talent Map that really rocks, because it has our unmistakable spin.

—MIKE

Our Sieve Analysis/Talent Map concept is rooted in the construction industry, but it could be adapted by any organization to apply right-brained thinking to setting standards for hiring and career development, as well as determining who flows through the ranks into leadership roles. Every organization needs programs or standards to vet new hires, set work expectations, and produce leaders who are devoted to its brand and goals.

In constructing our sieve, we purposely created tighter screens than our competitors would use. In other words, we set higher expectations, even at the entry level. The wording for those expectations distinctly reflects our approach. Instead of spelling out skills, it says the applicant "recognizes what he/she doesn't know and is eager to learn." As we get into the third-level sieve that's leading into team leadership, the skills expectation is that the applicant "has solid relationships and knows how to navigate social situations extremely well." The sieve matrix visually helps people to understand what it takes to get into the door and flow through the organization into different positions.

We took one more step and displayed our expectations in a right-brained version of the matrix. It doesn't just say we need someone to handle a large workload, but instead says they must be "willing to put one hundred pounds in their fifty-pound bag." Describing someone willing to do any task regardless of job title, we say we're looking for someone who "takes out the trash with a smile." The vivid language makes clear this is not just some corporate boilerplate. Job candidates can envision what's expected of them and determine where they fall in that sieve. We are clearly articulating that—beyond the basic job responsibilities—we expect employees to support the company's mission and values, and what that support looks like. If they are being honest with themselves, they won't be left wondering why they didn't get a job or get promoted.

We urge readers to come up with their own graphical representation and wordings of their expectations to fit their industry. Expectations should be out in the workplace on posters or on the company's internal website—not just used by executives in employee reviews and job interviews. The value of clearly stating expectations has been thoroughly documented in management books. One that influenced us was *Good to Great: Why Some Companies Make the Leap ... and Others Don't* by Jim C. Collins.

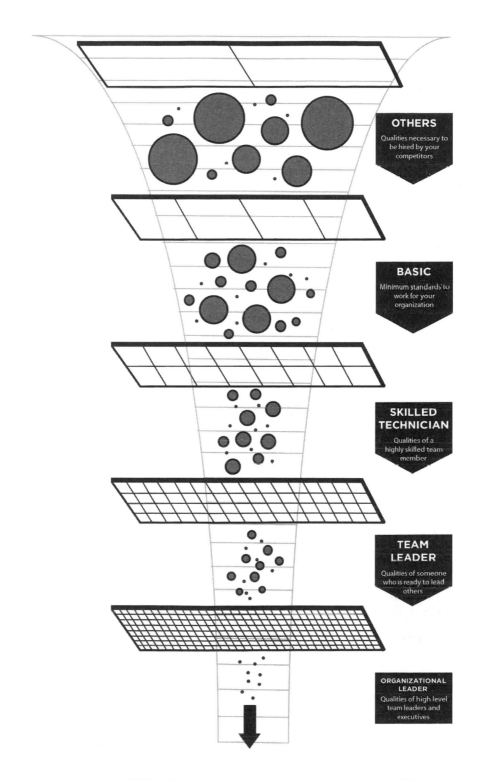

OTHERS
Qualities necessary to be hired by your competitors

BASIC
Minimum standards to work for your organization

SKILLED TECHNICIAN
Qualities of a highly skilled team member

TEAM LEADER
Qualities of someone who is ready to lead others

ORGANIZATIONAL LEADER
Qualities of high level team leaders and executives

We draw a lot of our leadership practices from what we read. But we've taken the heart and the right-brained side of leadership to energize our implementation of those practices. We constantly look for ways to show employees how they can do things in an unmistakable way. Just getting the job done leaves your bosses satisfied enough to give you a paycheck and your clients satisfied enough to pay the bills, but it doesn't create anything that's unmistakable. It doesn't create an unmistakable employee. It doesn't make you an unmistakable vendor to your client and, ultimately, doesn't make you unmistakable in your market. We like to say that a client who is only "satisfied" is one misstep away from moving on to the competition. We choose to perform at a level where a misstep or two can be easily forgiven.

> *Just getting the job done leaves your bosses satisfied enough to give you a paycheck and your clients satisfied enough to pay the bills, but it doesn't create anything that's unmistakable.*

AN EMPLOYEE'S PERSONAL BRAND

We're trying to get people to build their own *personal* brand that reflects our *corporate* brand. They should be doing the right thing when no one's looking, and be driven to be award-worthy. On a personal level, that might mean being worthy of an award like Neighbor of the Year in their community. There are ways in a workplace to inspire that kind of personal achievement.

We created a memorable example one time when we had a company-wide meeting scheduled at our office. We set a soft drink can outside with a $50 bill hidden inside it. It looked like litter just outside our main entryway. We watched from upstairs as employees passed by without picking it up, until one young man threw it into a trash can. We retrieved it, brought it into the meeting and asked, "Who threw this can away?" The young man raised his hand, and I shook the can so that the $50 bill came out. I handed it to him and explained to the staff that his action represented our company's brand of doing the right thing even when you think nobody is watching. Promoting and reinforcing that thinking is important in a company that sends people out to work solo or unsupervised, often hundreds or thousands of miles away.

Our chief operating officer, Tony Roussey, tells a story about a client that had a reputation for testing contractors by hiring them for a small job. The client's philosophy was, "If you can't do a simple $5,000 project well, why would I give you a $5 million job?" So even though we all want the big account, we have to train our people to understand that even the smallest of jobs are just as important. They may even be more important, because without these small projects being executed flawlessly, we will never get the larger ones. Our company does two thousand projects a year, and only two dozen or so are the big, shiny multimillion-dollar projects that people fixate on. Our success depends on our people doing a good job on *all* projects, the majority of which are under $100,000.

A VISUAL CONNECTION TO BUSINESS GOALS

To better communicate our business goals to all employees, we came up with a process of individual growth planning we call uMapping.

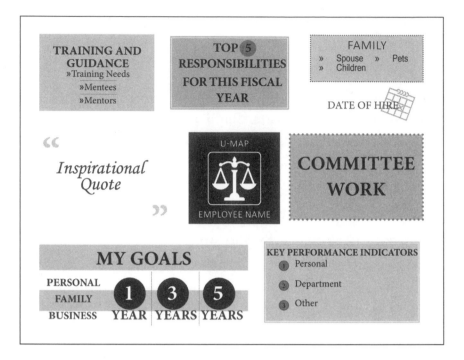

The uMap concept was developed as a thesis project in an innovative-methods course we participated in. Previously we didn't have an effective way of getting our people to buy into our annual business plans or the strategic plans we put together every few years. These strategic plans, about ten pages long, contained good ideas but generated no companywide passion. Similarly, the business plans ran on for fifty pages and mostly sat in some executives' desks. We reduced both the strategic plan and the business plan to five, eleven by seventeen-inch pages with few words and lots of graphics.

Having to depict an initiative in a picture or two is a real challenge. But we found that once we told the story of what each graphic stood for, the visual communication helped people remember and led to more buy-in. We might have a little picture of two baskets, one full of eggs and one empty. It is easier for people to remember that we're worried about having our eggs in one basket than to remember that our business plan droned on for five pages about the need for diversification.

Our next step was to get every person in our company to make their own eleven by seventeen-inch graphical uMap showing their goals and their individual responsibility for the company's goals. Their uMaps also display some personal information and their unique brand icon. Just as we would put the company logo on our strategic plan, we challenge them to create their own brand icon that represents who they are at their core. They use icons, clip art, and stock photos freely available online, and we provide an easy-to-use template for this exercise, which challenges them to describe themselves from a right-brained perspective. Other sections of the uMap include their commitment statement on what they're going to do that year for the company, in addition to their personal, family, and business goals for one, three, and five years. The uMap includes key performance indicators, but it is more than a job-assessment tool. Because we believe we should get to know the people we work with beyond just their business lives, we ask each of them to include a favorite quote that motivates him or her.

This one sheet of paper says, in a way that is visual and easy to read, "I understand where the company is going and how I can help it get there. The company understands how I'm wired, what's meaningful to me, and what my hopes and desires are. Together, we will make each other successful." That may sound idealistic, but after a few years of doing this uMapping, we have found it to be a game-changer. We better understand our people's hopes, desires, and aspirations. They are asked to talk with people around them (both above and below) to discover what others think their top five responsibilities are. When you align this broader perspective with a business and strategic plan, it's incredible how you can hone in on an individual's most impactful top-five priorities that support others' needs and the businesses goals.

Our people are collaborating with each other to make sure their uMaps are on target. It is the agenda for periodic meetings that managers have with their direct reports. It is the map for success for both them and the company. It shows how they might move through the organization. And it is updated every year. We laminate everyone's uMap, reflecting how it is something of value that will be handled and used repeatedly. They can put it up on the wall or use it like a placemat on a desk, but the important thing is it's not just filed away, forgotten, or discarded.

A publicly traded company may still need to generate the kind of detailed and formal business plan we used to create. But to communicate that plan throughout a workforce, our graphical, storytelling, warmer approach makes the vision much easier to understand and remember. Of course, many organizations have mission statements that concisely communicate what drives them. For us, the graphic with a smile and a dollar sign visually communicates our belief that if we see smiles on the faces of our clients, employees, and everyone else we interact with, the money will follow, and we will be more profitable. We have fifteen years of data so far to back up that belief.

A BLUEPRINT FOR SUCCESS

We came to realize that how well we onboarded employees directly correlated with their later success with us. For our company to grow, we had to do a great job training and connecting new employees to the company and its people. We were concerned that careless onboarding could also lead to higher turnover. Then we had a new employee join us with some HR background and some ideas that he put into his uMap. His goal was to help to develop a stronger onboarding program that was unmistakably E&V.

The Blueprint for Success Program, executed and championed by that employee, has improved our system of coaching new hires and helping them build numerous relationships with coworkers as early as possible. The basis of this system is using a wide sampling of current employees to teach new employees small lessons and procedures in a one-on-one environment. The program gives new employees a resource if they need future assistance. The program is also a great vetting tool for catching a bad hire. In an unmistakable culture, your people can quickly identify an individual's true colors, which may not have been obvious at an interview.

Another program resulted from uMap discussions of employees' personal and family goals: some of our middle-aged field managers mentioned that they wanted to have wills drawn up. We discovered that quite a few of our employees had no will, because it's a scary thing for some and an expense that's easy to put off. We worked out a deal with our corporate attorney to get those wills done for only $250 each, which we agreed to pay if they completed the process within sixty days. That offer put a fire under them, helped several employees check off a uMap goal, and we believe made us heroes with their spouses.

Some employees are more hesitant than others to show their vulnerability and share personal and family goals. We encourage them to be specific, because it is more effective to say, "I want to lose twenty-five pounds" than to say, vaguely, "I want to lose weight." Some will be very specific about a goal as personal as weight loss. We explain that the better we understand their day-to-day goals, the better we can support them in what they are trying to do. If that weight-loss goal involves going to a swimming class every Thursday morning, we can agree they'll be in a little late on Thursdays. Sharing personal goals leads to camaraderie and mutual support. One employee with a weight-loss goal had a colleague offer to be his gym buddy.

When personal goals involve training or a college degree, we can help them hold themselves accountable to that commitment and find the right programs. Some companies see a clear return on investment when they help pay for employee education. At other companies, executives resist paying because they fear the money will be wasted if the employee leaves. Since our company culture values having smart people with good attitudes, we support continuous education. We are regularly supporting two to four people pursuing advanced degrees or training, and we have gone as far as paying the full cost of an MBA for about ten managers—no strings attached. We're not saying, "If you leave within three years, pay us back," because we find they are grateful and none have left. We see that employees we invest in at this level feel highly valued and appreciative of our investment in them. They tend to be "bleeding our corporate-blue colors" with this level of commitment from us. We believe it improves retention dramatically.

For our left-brained readers who are wondering how we could justify such a large expenditure, the answer is simple: in our business, a smart decision by a better-educated project manager can easily save the $25,000 we might have spent on tuition. But really, our right-brained approach is to avoid a monetary calculation and ask, "What is the right thing to do?"

> Elzinga & Volkers prides itself on assisting all employees who wish to continue their education. I (Mike) often share how we fully reimburse our employees for the cost of their master's degrees. After telling many other companies about this program, I was informed that one of our employees only requested 50 percent reimbursement—since that is what the policy stated when she started her MBA program. I decided it was only right to correct this and reimbursed her for the other 50 percent of her tuition expenses. A couple weeks after her reimbursement, I had the opportunity to talk to her parents and hear their reactions.

Scott and Peggy's Perspective:

After work one day, my daughter called me and asked if I had a few minutes because she had something important to tell me. She asked if her dad was there and to get him and put the call on speakerphone because she wanted to talk to the both of us together. I got my husband and we were initially a little worried. When your daughter calls and prefaces her story with these details and requests, your mind goes in a lot of different and concerning directions.

She started off by saying she got a letter in the mail from Mike—not a card, an actual letter—and wondered why it was mailed and not handed to her at work. As parents, we were equally confused. Then she started reading the letter, word for word, to us. Her voice started out quivery, overwhelmed with the contents of the letter. She went on to read that E&V was going to reimburse her for the remaining 50 percent of the tuition expenses surrounding her master's degree. This was completely out of the blue as she graduated three years prior.

As parents, we are endlessly grateful to E&V for thinking so highly of our daughter and her education. We are amazed that, after so many years, they remembered our daughter's expenses and wanted to correct their error and make sure our daughter was treated equally. We know how much they appreciate both her as a person as well as the work she is doing. Their act of generosity shows how great of a company E&V is and how much they value our daughter.

We also have a dozen internal training programs, taught by employees who volunteer their time and expertise. A lot of companies have found that type of program fosters a culture of being passionate about sharing knowledge. An employee will be a teacher in one class and a student in another class, which promotes mutual respect and the idea of giving back. Employees are more engaged when listening to their peers than they would be if the course were online or taught by an outsider. Another benefit is that employees are more confident in learning some new software or skill when they know the instructor will be around to answer questions later.

Employees are mostly forthcoming about their personal and family goals because our company built trust and respect among managers and workers before we started the uMap program. Company leaders disclose their goals, setting the general expectation for how much information is okay to be shared. The leadership has to be as vulnerable as we want the employees to be.

Mike Discusses His First uMap

The first year we made uMaps, my icon included an infinity symbol as part of a logo that had a smiley face, to convey my goal of putting a smile on the face of everyone all the time. My personal quote was from Yoda in *Star Wars*—"Do or do not. There is no try." We had two management meetings, both involving about twenty people discussing their uMaps and sharing what their icons and quotes meant to them. The discussions helped develop intimacy in the group as we learned more about how each of us is wired. By the end of the meetings, everyone could remember which logo belonged to which manager. A picture was more memorable than just listening to people talk about themselves.

Other companies have their managers take personality-profile tests, and then gather to discuss the results. One test called DiSC promises to measure your dominance, influence, steadiness, and conscientiousness so you and your colleagues can better understand your work style and how to build more effective relationships. The uMap serves a similar purpose but ties in more to company goals and accountability because it is a laminated physical reminder throughout the year. The few employees who struggled with developing their uMap or who resisted the process were not good hires, because they can't be vulnerable, can't share, and can't envision how they help bring us success.

In onboarding employees and working with them each year to set goals, we have come up with clear, graphical programs to help them visualize how they fit into our vision and brand. The programs help them find and develop their strengths and help us identify leaders. Our people get to know each other and work together better, and the leadership grows to care more about the individuals at a deeper level. What follows naturally, as you'll learn in the next chapter, is an employee-centric company culture.

Chapter Five Toolbox

UMAP

We talked about uMaps earlier in the chapter and how powerful they can be in connecting your employees to the organization's goals and expectations. Start by communicating your organization's goals and purpose to your team members. Give these team members the uMap framework and allow them to get creative in completing the sections and connecting them to your company's core purpose. Using effective visual design, format the uMap into a one-page graph similar to the provided template.

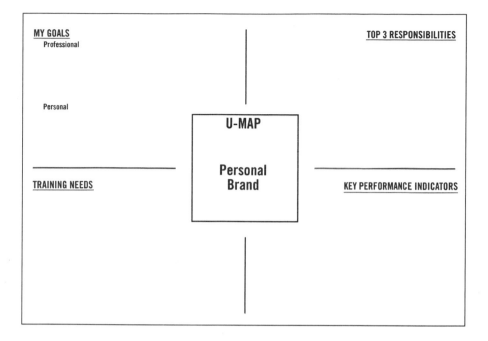

CHAPTER 6

MAINTAINING AN EMPLOYEE-CENTRIC CULTURE

The true test of a company's culture is how it endures trying times. A big test for us came when our chief operating officer received a shocking medical diagnosis. Tony had breast cancer, a disease that affects relatively few men. He had chemotherapy, radiation, and surgery during his three-year recovery process. The illness hit him hard, of course, but it also hit our company emotionally. Being the tough individual that he is, Tony never missed a day in the office during his treatment and thrived on the support he received from his work family. Once Tony was cancer-free, we decided to surprise him with a "Celebrate Life" road trip.

—MIKE

The executive committee basically kidnapped Tony with the aid of his family and took him from Michigan to Chicago. One of Tony's three adult sons lives in our area and helped plan the trip.

We also decided to celebrate the preciousness of father-son relationships by inviting our dads, so seven of us rode in two cars. We had Tony clear his schedule for a few days of "important meetings" starting with a six o'clock breakfast at a restaurant. His wife packed a bag and gave it to us. Once he was in the car, we hit the road and did a bunch of fun stuff along the way like driving high-speed go-karts. To cap it off, we attended a Chicago Cubs baseball game.

Maybe a left-brained executive would take issue with using company money for a surprise road trip with fathers and sons. In our right-brained thinking, anticipating fun surprises as part of our work life creates a unique energy and excitement in our company. Blending our personal and work lives and instilling pride in our fathers are valuable goals, and it makes sense for a company to recognize its core leadership in special ways. So, we have made such surprises part of our routine.

> *In our right-brained thinking, anticipating fun surprises as part of our work life creates a unique energy and excitement in our company.*

When Tony turned sixty, we surprised him and David Novakoski—Mike's father—and Joe, now our VP of operations, with a surprise trip to Las Vegas. David happened to be turning seventy-five, so we celebrated two major milestones and recognized the extended E&V family with this trip, which included our wives as well as the fathers and sons.

Recently while attending a convention, we took a break and wandered into a high-end men's store, where an expensive sports jacket caught the eye of one of our talented project managers. We encouraged him to try it on, and we could see he really liked it but would not have bought it for himself. So, we bought it for him.

"Really? Why are you doing this?" he asked.

"It's because we care about you. We want you to feel good, and we want you to understand how much we appreciate you."

On another business trip where two female executives were with us, the four of us visited a Lululemon store and each got to buy one item at the company's expense. It was a way to have fun together and for the women in an admittedly male-dominated industry to lead us into an after-work experience that they enjoyed.

The business case for such gifts is that they are much more memorable than a $1,000 bonus check. Whether it's a jacket, yoga pants, or a round of go-karting, the gift recognizes the uniqueness of the individual. Picking it out together is an experience they remember every time they wear the item or look at pictures in a photo album from the trip.

AT THE TOP OF OUR LADDER: SAFETY

A more consequential way we show we care about our employees involves safety. A lot of construction companies regard safety as an unfortunate business cost. They disdain the Occupational Safety and Health Administration (OSHA) as a police force that exists to make our lives miserable. Their approach to OSHA is to avoid it when possible and argue when confronted. But with Tony's leadership, we have developed an employee-centric understanding

> *The health, safety, and welfare of each of our people is more important than anything else.*

in our company: the health, safety, and welfare of each of our people is more important than anything else. We've spent more money than our competitors would on some jobs because we were scrupulously following—and often going above and beyond—mandates of our state OSHA. At first, we worried about the higher cost affecting our competitiveness. But our mindset gradually became, "We have to do it because it's the right thing to do. It's our moral obligation as an employer to make sure that our men and women go home safely and in one piece at the end of each day."

Along the way, we found that emphasizing safety made us a stronger competitor, because it improved our entire company culture. We started simply by offering monthly meetings with top executives talking about different safety topics with every single employee, from receptionists to accounting clerks to the seasoned tradespeople. We believe *everyone* must understand our safety culture. Later we realized our people were more engaged when we gave the speaking assignment to a team of two or three managers and tradespeople who work in the field. We asked them to do some research, look up statistics, and work with the marketing department to put their information into a visual presentation. The dynamic changed when our people took ownership of the safety program. Realizing that one day they'd be the ones up there talking about hardhats, fall prevention, or dealing with cold weather, the audience listens intently.

A Few Words from Mike about "Annoying" Rules

OSHA has dozens of rules just about ladders, and very specific requirements for what our government calls "personal fall-arrest systems." A worker who is six feet off the ground has to be tied in securely with a body harness. A lot of people in our industry find the requirement annoying. They say, "I'm just going to go up this stepladder to fix a ceiling tile. I don't need to be tied off." Our training helps them understand why the rules are not a nuisance, that many people are injured—some killed or paralyzed—in falls as short as six feet.

Concern about safety became a standard in our hiring and a constant presence at our job sites. The managers we are looking for—hungry, humble, and smart—are not the type to enforce rules out of meanness or lack of flexibility. But they will enforce a safety rule—such as 100 percent use of hardhats—because they want their people to get home to their children. To reinforce the emotional appeal of our emphasis on safety, we put together a coloring contest for the children of our employees who wanted to participate. The top of the page said, "Why it's important for my _____ (mom, dad, grandma, grandpa) to be home at night for me." The drawings showed kids being tucked into bed, reading stories at night, or being pushed on a swing. Kids could add their own favorite: "My dad plays catch with me," "My dad helps me with my homework," etc. Winners received prizes and a trip to a minor-league baseball game. More important, we laminated the drawings and our people posted them on office doors and in job-site trailers. Seeing a hand-drawn Crayola picture from a six-year-old describing why safety is important to his or her is much more impactful than the "100 Percent Hard-Hat Job Site" sign next to it on the trailer wall.

Our safety program really went into high gear when we rolled out our Alive 365® annual event for trade contractors. We'll go into detail about that training in chapter 8, but our point here is that we pushed our programs, including the coloring contest, outside our organization to increase its impact. The industry responded well, and the safety program won a top national award in March 2018 from the Associated Builders and Contractors, a 21,000-member trade group.

A RIPPLE-EFFECT IDEA

We're always trying to give our corporate culture an Unmistakably E&V spin, which means we are looking for visual ways to communicate. Business books are loaded with acronyms, but we embraced one we thought would be particularly memorable: **ABS**, for **Artifacts, Beliefs, and Stories**. The artifacts are the things you see, attention-getters that express a company's culture. In our building, for example, we have autographed boxing gloves from heavyweight legend Evander Holyfield that represent the "lean, 165-pound prizefighter" outlook that carried us through the Great Recession. You'll find other examples throughout the book you're holding of our company's artifacts, beliefs, and stories.

> *Business books are loaded with acronyms, but we embraced one we thought would be particularly memorable: ABS, for artifacts, beliefs, and stories.*

We thought that for our company to be solid, we needed to have a strong core. And if you think about the physical core of a strong person, it's those much-coveted six-pack abs. We've been playing on that fitness metaphor by saying, "We have strong ABS." But like an insecure bodybuilder, we are always checking the mirror and asking, "How are our ABS looking?" Are they defined, noticeable, impressive?

A·B·S
Artifacts, Beliefs, Stories

ARE YOU FIT FOR BUSINESS?

One of our favorite artifacts is an air siren that we sound when we get a big job. One of our beliefs, discussed in chapter 3, is that our managers should realize when employees are owed more than what's spelled out in the manual of standard operating procedures. Our stories, like the birthday surprises we described earlier in the chapter, become part of our culture.

PLEASANT SURPRISES

We decided to become more intentional about making pleasant surprises part of how we do business. We noticed that in the last weeks of a construction project, the owner's excited to move in and often forgets all of the hard work and accomplishments of getting to move in day. To remind them formally, we came up with the idea of sending a letter recapping what we have done—the heroic accomplishments, the schedule improvements, creative ideas for cost savings, and so on. We call it our Pleasant Surprise Letter because it acknowledges successes achieved together as a team. Then we express appreciation for the business and say we look forward to being the contractor on their next job. We not only get repeat business but also are able to elicit video testimonials from proud owners in their new buildings. They know what to say because they have a Pleasant Surprise Letter in their hands spelling out exactly what we did for them. By contrast, many contractors surprise owners at the end of the job with a list of extra charges they've incurred, which sours the relationship.

Later we expanded the idea of pleasant surprises to better recognize our people internally. We began sending thank-you notes to a spouse whose husband or wife was away working long hours. We might include a gift card and say, "It would be great if you could take her out to dinner, and don't tell her that we gave you the money." Of course, they'll tell their spouses what the company did. More important, if the employee gets a job offer from our competitor, the spouse who is part of the decision is a raving fan of E&V and will remind the employee just how well the company treats them. A great surprise is when we can send a perfect gift because we listen to employees talk about things they want, and we write it down, so we can refer to it even years later.

Our right-brained thinking led us to apply the concept of pleasant surprises to a broader effort to produce constant, small, positive interactions. We called this the E&V Experience. It doesn't necessarily cost money. When our workers are on a job site, they are trained to do little "not-my-job" things like hold a door open or pick up litter. Small positive impressions over time help balance or even outweigh a negative experience that may happen because nobody's perfect. If you are a small contractor or startup and don't have the resources to buy gifts and run training programs, you can still do small things for your clients and recap them in a Pleasant Surprise Letter. If you don't have time to write a letter, just list them on the invoice as extra services for $0.00.

Mike Recalls Some Pleasant Surprises

An audit turned up an error in which we had nine months earlier billed a client for an item we bought for the job, but then returned. We sent the client a check for $1,872, a pleasant surprise for them since most contractors only issue credits if the client catches the error. I got a pleasant surprise myself once after I had some work done on my home. A year later, the contractor mailed me a package of batteries for the smoke detectors with a reminder to change them each year. Such gestures create loyal customers who provide referrals.

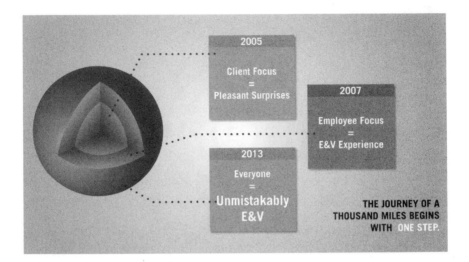

The E&V Experience turned out to be a step on our journey to the company culture we now call Unmistakably E&V. It evolved from occasional gestures like holding the door open to constantly looking for ways to apply our approach to every business and personal relationship that we have. It developed to a point where we were so totally different from others in our industry that it was unmistakable. Our devotion to a particular way of living our business life, and our commitment to acting in a certain way are deeply held beliefs (the 'B' in our ABS). We can joke that we have a company CULTure, because we don't have any of the negative aspects associated with cults.

Our "cult" is built around a shared belief system, not a leader, and the philosophy is ingrained enough in the company that everybody ministers to it. New employees get caught up in our beliefs and excited when they realize they are going to have a much different experience than they've had in any other job. A lot of companies post slogans around the office without their people really buying in to the ideas. Our people act constantly on our shared beliefs without having to be reminded.

Given our demographics in western Michigan, Christmas is celebrated and highly anticipated by everyone at our company. A great reflection of our beliefs is the way we put together gifts for each family of our office workers and senior field managers to open on Christmas morning. Everything inside is chosen specifically for the family, because we know them and their interests. Cards and personalized letters handwritten by the CEO in silver and gold markers express our thanks to each of our employees for what he or she has individually contributed to our company success that year. Some might question whether a CEO should be spending more than twelve hours hand-writing these messages, no two alike. It is absolutely worth the time making a connection with all these people. We don't see the value in a generic letter that has been photocopied and signed electronically.

Mike Describes a Holiday Gift that Literally Headed South

I knew our CFO, Grace Silva, was driving to Florida with her husband and son for Christmas, so I packaged travel gifts that would make the trip more fun. There were things to occupy them in the car, and envelopes marked to be opened when they crossed various state lines.

> One contained a $100 bill for her son, Bennett, to spend during the vacation. When he opened it, Grace texted me a picture showing Bennett with a huge smile holding up what he said was his first $100 bill. The upshot is that they knew they were still on our minds, even while she was off the clock and far away.

We know our people put a lot of hours and energy into maintaining our Unmistakably E&V belief system. Those efforts often go above and beyond the jobs they are paid to perform. So, little thank-you gifts from time to time are the right thing to do, and we try to make them memorable experiences. Other business owners think they are treating their people more fairly and not playing favorites if everybody gets the same thing. They are afraid to do anything special for a high performer because they think they have to do it for everyone. In our philosophy, we want to be treated as unique and unmistakable, so we treat others the same way. We don't want to treat our employees like a commodity. Every organization has key people. We have gotten to know ours on a personal level, and we are rewarding them in a personal way.

NO PARTICIPATION TROPHIES

We're not a blue-ribbon-for-everybody kind of company. We reward top performance differently than standard performance, because that's what we want out of our business. Of course, we challenge ourselves to fill all positions with top performers. That's not easy, but over time, with intentionality, it's possible. Spoiling everyone because they are all top performers would be our best-case scenario. We want our clients to pay a premium for a higher level of service, and we should pay a premium to our employees that perform at that high level.

That philosophy raises the question of work/life balance. We're in a world now where punching in from eight to five o'clock and turning off work outside of those hours is unrealistic. We're getting work email on our cell phones on Sunday morning before church, and our people are looking at their social media and handling personal matters from the office. It's funny now to think that companies once thought they could block that type of activity. Our approach is to respect and trust that the employees are getting their work done. We want them to be award-worthy at work, at home, and in their communities. If they share our belief system, they are asking themselves, "How do I make others central in my life? How can I be the best version of myself when it comes to my neighbors and my family?" So, they need time to be a unique and memorable husband, wife, or significant other.

For example, one of our people was helping his daughter refinish an old desk she bought for her dorm room. He stapled a $100 bill and a note underneath the drawer, because he knew he would get a call from her when the stress of college set in, probably around midterms. He thought it would be nice then to send her on a little treasure hunt to look for a special message from her dad, and more usefully, some spending money.

FINDING A COMPANY CREED

A getaway from work led me, Mike, to our *company creed*. I was in Mobile, Alabama, for a meeting of the YPO Construction Industry Forum, where noncompeting members share best practices. We all went to lunch at an oyster bar called Wintzell's. It was decorated floor to ceiling with funny quotes that employees heard Mr. Wintzell say over the decades. They painted them on white signs and screwed them to the wall. We enjoyed reading them. On the way out, I noticed a longer statement from Mr. Wintzell about the mutually beneficial relationship between him and his town. It was posted on a large piece of plywood by the back door. I took a picture and shared it a few weeks later at my company planning retreat. We broke into groups and each used Mr. Wintzell's words as inspiration to write statements about what our company owes employees and what the employees in turn owe the company. The groups brought tremendous energy to the exercise, and when we shared our results I was proud and very misty eyed about what they came up with. We took the best of the wording and made a company creed.

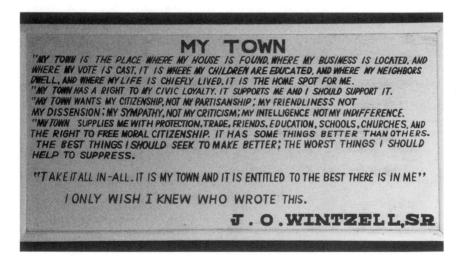

I wrote a blog item about the exercise, and through the magic of an automated Internet search, Wintzell's Oyster House picked up on it. Soon a package arrived from Alabama with Wintzell's shirts and hats and a letter saying, "Awesome article. We're so proud." It was fun how it happened, but we took the idea of a creed seriously. A lot of companies produce a formal summary of goals as a mission statement. We were trying to capture our belief system and how we feel about the company. A creed better connected to our right-brained desire for a deeper, more emotional doctrine—a covenant between the employee and the company.

EV Company Creed

My company is the place where my talents are allowed to shine, where my work family is located, and where my vote has impact. It is where my life is enriched, where my children aspire to work, and where my neighbors wish they could be. It is a second home for me.

My company has a right to my loyalty, and a right to my dedication.

My company supports me, and I support it.

My company wants my name, not my number; my creative ideas, not my blind obedience; my best efforts, not my minimum requirements; and my safety, not just my productivity.

My company supplies me with a sense of pride; inspiration to advance my career; the flexibility to be there for my kids; empowerment to make change happen; continuous training and growth opportunities; security for my family; and the challenge to be like no other.

My company does some things better than others. The best things I should seek to reinforce and the worst things I should help to rebuild.

Take it all in. It is my company and it is Unmistakably E&V.

We've described how our company developed a shared belief system that made us unmistakable in how we look after, recognize, and reward our employees and treat everyone in our personal and business lives. You have heard it from us, and above in the company creed, you heard it directly from our employees. In the next chapter we show the business advantages of differentiating ourselves from the competition—becoming an oddity to avoid being a commodity.

Chapter Six Toolbox

ABS: ARTIFACTS, BELIEFS, STORIES

We've discussed how corporate culture is comprised of three main components which we refer to as your corporate ABS. For this toolbox, take an inventory of your ABS and determine which areas may be weak.

Artifacts: These are specific physical items in your office that, when described, represent a value that your company holds.

_____

_____

_____

_____

_____

_____

Beliefs: The ideas and values that you hold true even when it costs you time or money.

_____

_____

_____

_____

_____

_____

Stories: Anecdotes and examples that your leaders commonly use to communicate the company's beliefs and values.

_____

_____

_____

_____

_____

_____

Are you fit for business?

CHAPTER 7

THE JOURNEY FROM COMMODITY TO ODDITY

We had the honor of being named general contractor for an expansion of one of our hometown's great institutions, the Western Theological Seminary. The seminary hired the big international design company Stantec, whose architects are very experienced at this type of work. The seminary project owners and their architects came to our office to discuss the expansion goals. That's when we broke out our bins full of pipe cleaners, Styrofoam balls, Popsicle sticks, cardboard, glue, and other arts-and-crafts materials.

—JOHN

You know from the previous chapters that we believe visual symbols are more powerful than words when discussing goals. So, sometimes we do a visualization exercise in our conference room to kick off a project. We break into teams, each with somebody from the owner's team, somebody from the architecture firm, and somebody from our company, to build three-dimensional models to represent things that would make the project a success. These are not scale models of the whole project, but visual representations of the project's core values. The teams explain what those models mean. Then it is much easier to discuss and agree on the principles that should guide the project, and to have a common language.

Most contractors would not have representatives of an international architecture firm playing with Popsicle sticks in a conference room. But we have found that the use of abstract objects in the exercise helps switch on right-brained thinking, which can lead to creative solutions to left-brained challenges, such as working within a budget. We could have just left it to the seminary project owners and their architects to work through their issues and priorities. But with our right-brained approach, we're an oddity, not a commodity. We lean into challenges, adding value beyond just building the building, even when it means stepping outside the normal role for a general contractor.

> *With our right-brained approach, we're an oddity, not a commodity. We lean into challenges, adding value beyond just building the building, even when it means stepping outside the normal role for a general contractor.*

Companies in commodity industries get caught in a race to the bottom when they compete only on price. General contractors especially face pressure to submit the lowest bid and figure out later how to manage costs enough to still make money. Our decision not to play that game has taken many forms. We created a unique Quality Standards Program. We focused on safety, which resulted in more than ten years with no lost-time accidents, a feat unheard of in our industry. We take care of our employees' work/life balance and devote time and resources to showing respect for their families. Those practices make us an oddity in our industry, in the good sense that we have workers who do their jobs like no others.

We get some strange looks when we haul out the arts-and-crafts bins, but we explain that our exercise works better than sitting around writing words on a whiteboard. Words can be abstract. What does someone mean when he says something in the project "has to have balance"?

Four teams of three can brainstorm and get creative in our exercise to come up with ideas to fulfill needs and avoid costs. For example, the seminary was building a learning center that needed a lot of library book-storage space. One idea for shrinking the space and cost was electronic book storage. If the same twelve people sat around the conference table, some would dominate the conversation, and others might be reluctant to interrupt with their ideas. The different models produced by the four teams at the seminary project meeting offered more of a diversity of ideas than we could get from a left brained, traditional brainstorming session. We left the session with a better understanding of what the client wanted, and a visual representation in our heads. We also took pictures of the models to share with others later.

Sometimes people don't realize the energy our right-brained approach brings to a meeting until they experience it. For example, at our first meeting with clients overseeing a Catholic church project, we started out by saying, "Tell us about a fond memory of your faith growing up." That might seem to be an odd request from a general contractor. But one by one we went around the room and people told stories about the church they grew up in.

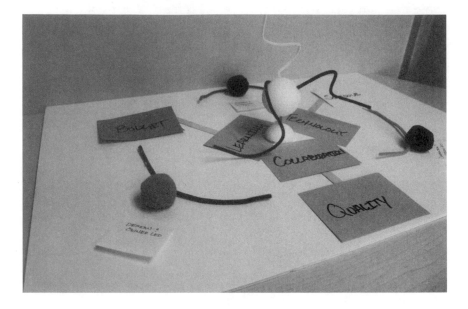

One woman said her dad always had trouble wrangling the family to get out of the house on time Sunday morning to get to church—and they had to cross a lake by boat to get there! One time they rushed into church several minutes late and found space only in the front pews. That made it especially embarrassing when they realized they were all sitting there still wearing their life jackets. The group laughed together, and through some other stories realized they had past connections they hadn't even known about, even though they were in the same parish for decades. The human interaction helped us ease into our more technical and difficult business discussions. We risked raised eyebrows with our request for stories, but the end reaction was, "It was a great way to start the meeting."

This kind of right-brained approach can work in any industry. We think it's especially effective in commoditized industries such as construction. Contractors traditionally have acquired work by bidding against other contractors. The low bidder gets awarded the contract, which turns all the contractors into commodities. Other industries have similar issues with reverse auctions, target pricing, and whatever other devices corporate purchasers come up with to drive prices down.

Notice that we didn't say the purchasers were trying to "drive costs down." Some people use the words price and cost interchangeably. *Price* is what you pay at the time of the transaction; *cost* is what you end up incurring over the life of that purchase. We often make the distinction, because cost over the life of a building should be a much bigger consideration than the initial price. Lifetime cost can be the main consideration even in a small purchase, such as a battery or light bulb. Everybody knows the cheap ones don't last as long. Smart consumers are unfazed at the price of LED bulbs being three times as much as incandescent bulbs when the buyers are aware that the more expensive bulbs burn forty times as long and use a fraction of the power. The calculations are more complicated for a project in which the construction manager's fee is a percentage of the overall cost of the project. For example, our fee could be 3 percent vis-à-vis the competitor's 2.75 percent. But if we're better at expense avoidance, and if we create a longer-lasting, lower-maintenance building, the short- and long-term savings would make choosing the lower fee the wrong decision. Additionally, we could finish a building or addition sooner, allowing the owner to make more money more quickly.

> ***Price*** *is what you pay at the time of the transaction;* ***cost*** *is what you end up incurring over the life of that purchase.*

Financial decision-makers in commercial situations are accountable for paying the lowest price and can't just dismiss a low bidder based on feelings or hunches. As general contractors, we feel the same pressure to get the best price when we seek vendors or bid out jobs to trade contractors. But we do run across vendors that have such a unique value proposition that it justifies a higher price. It happens when they've got a great reputation for quality and customer service, and their people are much more careful on the job and more attentive to detail than are other vendors. The more businesses differentiate themselves based on those traits, the less they will be commoditized. But the burden is on the vendors, not the buyers, to accentuate what they offer beyond a good price.

A Few Words from John about Quality Standards

In our industry, contractors are obligated professionally and legally to follow the architects' drawings and specifications. But even the best architects can miss small details in the complicated process of preparing construction drawings. They cannot anticipate every situation that may pop up, especially during a complex renovation or remodeling project. An unmistakable contractor with high quality standards won't allow something to be installed incorrectly and will maintain the project's functionality, be flexible, and add value even if the drawings don't specifically reflect it. These contractors will achieve this by having a collection of minimum-quality criteria for each trade, regardless of the drawings and specifications given by the architect. We call it our Quality Standards Manual®.

Think about the minimum-quality standards in your industry. Meeting or exceeding these standards will make you noticeably different from your competitors who are just trying to be the low-cost provider. Talk about these standards with your customers and share the risks of cutting corners. This conversation will plant a seed in your customers' minds when they are evaluating you against others in the marketplace.

When service providers seek our business, we're not impressed if everything they say is something we've heard from their competitors. We put them on the spot and ask, "What are the things that truly differentiate you from the others?" The response is usually something vague like, "We're really innovative," or, "We're very customer-focused." It has been surprising how few businesses—even including a marketing company that approached us recently—could tell us precisely what differentiated them. When we are asked what differentiates us, we give specific replies: we were named Michigan's Contractor of the Year two of the last four years, we have not had a lost-time accident in ten years, and so on.

Any organization can create distinctive, reputation-building programs. An idea we gave to the CEO of a nonprofit hospital was to invite a dozen recent patients in for a luncheon each month to ask what they liked and didn't like about the health service they received. The idea was that, within a year, this small community would have 144 people who would be talking to friends about how a hospital CEO had asked for their opinion, and more importantly, brag to their friends and family how the CEO bought them lunch! If the hospital acted on some of the advice, those changes would make a great story for the hospital to tell in newsletters or the media. The patient feedback also could drive new programming for the hospital.

Traditionally, some businesses and organizations like hospitals or nonprofits have rested on their laurels, but they are finding that people now can search out information more easily on their brand and reputation. Health insurers encourage patients to shop around. Parents have increasing options in many areas to choose among public, private, and charter schools. Which means that every organization must think about being competitive and unmistakable.

What It Means to Be a Commodity

A commodity, such as iron ore, doesn't vary with who produced it or who is selling it. When you taste a commodity item, such as a banana, you don't notice a distinctive flavor from one brand to the next. Commodity products and services are seen as interchangeable, which has the following negative effects.

- From the perspective of the seller or manufacturer:
  - constant pressure to cut costs
  - competing to achieve economies of scale
  - always worried about being undercut by competition
  - big companies can swallow or raid smaller ones
  - small companies perceived as having low overhead can beat larger, more adept companies
  - employee morale and loyalty suffer
- From the perspective of the buyer

- indifferent to factors other than price
- settling for "good-enough" products and impersonal service
- less likely to see innovation, creativity, and exceptional service
- consumer experience and brand loyalty suffer

What It Means to Be an Oddity

Companies known for their distinctive products and services don't get that way by following a formatted checklist, but they do have a few things in common:

- From the perspective of the seller or manufacturer:
  - focusing on quality over costs
  - doing the right thing even when nobody's looking
  - being more concerned about relationships than competition
  - employee-centric company culture
- From the perspective of the buyer:
  - attractive for reasons other than price
  - favored for exceptional quality and service
  - seen as creative, innovative, or unique
  - raving fan loyalty

A banana can have a Dole or Chiquita sticker, but still be a commodity. Those companies may advertise to try to make their brand attractive, but nobody could tell the difference in a blind taste-test. This lack of distinctiveness is more of a problem in some industries than others. As you have seen, we've given this issue a lot of thought, because we're in a transactional, adversarial industry with constant cost pressures resulting from commoditization. We must protect our margins but still need to charge the owners enough and pay the trade contractors enough to make sure the buildings we build are still standing in fifty or a hundred years.

Bidding at the level needed to make a fair profit became increasingly difficult when a reverse-auction process became popular in recent years. A developer of a big-box store, for example, might accept an unlimited number of construction bids in an open-ended process. Every general contractor could see the lowest current bid online and they could keep undercutting each other's bids until nobody wanted to go any lower. This race to the bottom disrespected contractors. Some of us refused to play the game, and those who did play often got hurt. Like gamblers at a casino who endure mounting losses, they would drop their bids too far, thinking they would somehow figure out later how to make it all work out. General contractors in turn could disrespect trade contractors by taking a bid from one and using that amount to ask another for a cheaper price. In our market, that "bid shopping" is considered unethical.

Focusing on quality and value flips the process. We want to be like the company that takes a commodity like gold and turns it into a beautiful collectible that's worth a lot more than the commodity price per ounce.

In the construction industry, if we take on a project before the owner has selected an architect, we can help the owner make qualitative comparisons by requesting information from each firm. Before we ask about price, we ask the architects to tell us their approach to the project. We ask what similar projects they have they done, the qualifications of the professionals they're going to assign to the project, and any other differentiation they bring. We then we do a scoring system based on just the qualitative information. In the meantime, the architects are getting to know us and the owner, our goals and expectations, and can factor this information into their prices. With this approach, the bids tend to be clustered close together, which makes us feel they are the right price for the right amount of service. The owner has also thought more about qualitative needs and is more likely to pay a little more for higher quality rather than feeling bias against a firm based on a high initial price. We may ask the owner to agree to various markups for labor and materials rather than one full-project price.

It's human nature to look at prices and rank them from low to high before digging into the other aspects. That price bias taints the ability to objectively analyze the quality of services. Thus, flipping the process whenever possible to get qualitative information first is a goal we have been pursuing and recommend to all types of organizations.

In our experience, we get a better deal in the long run if we have a well-defined project. In a business that can be adversarial and conflict-ridden, having a good contract with adequate profit margins reduces tension. With tension reduced, teams can better focus on achieving goals, not winning the next battle. Managers who have to meet unreasonable cost expectations are more likely to be yelling at workers. A company that has won a contract based on quality is in a better position to recruit talent and treat everyone more respectfully.

For example, let's say the plumbing work at a construction site is behind schedule. The general contractor could issue a written notice demanding additional manpower and threatening financial penalties. Our more respectful approach is to ask the owner of the plumbing company to come into our office and sit down to discuss what challenges he or she is having. Maybe the foreman got sick or his kid is in the hospital. Maybe we can help him catch up by providing some laborers to assist the plumbers. That solution might even cost less than paying a lawyer to enforce the contract.

Labor-union contracts, for all their value, unfortunately can be an impediment to our right-brained inclination to be flexible in devising solutions. We don't want to tell people they are a cog in a machine and can do only their specific task. We believe the individual value people bring to the job should define them and determine how they are compensated. In other words, we are saying that workers, like businesses, are better off if they are not commodities. When work of all sorts can be sent offshore to the lowest bidder, American jobs depend more on qualitative factors. Chasing the lowest cost of labor around the world may quickly end as developing nations become more developed and the price bias of offshoring recedes.

> *We like to say we're an oddity business, unafraid to be the antithesis of what people are expecting.*

What's the opposite of a commodity business? We like to say we're an oddity business, unafraid to be the antithesis of what people are expecting. Here are a few examples that we consider refreshing, if perhaps odd:

- Our leadership group decided to try equine-based learning, an idea that came from Mike's wife, Liz, and her passion for working with horses. We spent half a day with her on a ranch working with teams of horses to learn a new way of looking at teams working together and leadership. It was an eye opener and a unique experience that any team could learn from.

- Our top executives took up a dare from the staff and agreed to wear underwear on our heads if we won a particular contract. Our COO brought in a package of fresh tighty-whities, which we donned as headgear for the celebration.

- We had to ask an architect to redraw plans to make up for our failing to budget adequately for some work. When we found out the redrawing involved about $20,000 of additional time, we met with the architects over lunch and gave them a check to cover the extra time. They were blown away. This was a unique circumstance that we hope to never repeat—but it was the right thing to do in that situation.

- On April 15, the most stressful day for tax accountants, our CFO sent a $100 gourmet cookie basket to thank our outside auditors for their hard work. Most companies frankly resent how much they pay the big accounting firms for tax-audit work, so these people don't get a lot of love. We heard later they marched through the halls of their accounting firm carrying the cookie basket over their heads and bragged they had the best client.

We didn't think about this in advance, but accountants regularly discuss future capital projects with their clients, and because we stood out as a favorite, our happy auditors later gave us at least one referral worth a whole lot more than $100.

In his book, *Joy, Inc.*, Richard Sheridan of Menlo Innovations in Ann Arbor, Michigan, tells a story about thanking his office-cleaning company for the extra effort needed after a Christmas party. After he publicly shared his praise for the cleaning crew with his employees, his team took up a collection for the crew, with no prompting from him as the leader. I am sure that this extra attention to what can be considered a mundane service will have a great impact on the way that cleaning company views its client. Sheridan goes on to say, "When even your vendors align with your culture, you're on the right path."

We have some other practices that are not odd but distinguish us from other companies. We spend a considerable amount of time and money on safety, as mentioned previously and in the next chapter. We produce a quality-standards manual for each job, handing the owner and architect a thick binder that is above and beyond what they would normally request or receive. The document encapsulates everything we've learned from experience and the little things that concern us as perfectionists.

We have covered various ways we differentiate ourselves from the competition and focus on quality and value versus price to avoid the downsides of being a commodity. As an oddity company we celebrate successes versus blaming others when things are bad. We don't accept the status quo. We do things the hard way, literally paying for mistakes versus making excuses. Our leadership can admit to mistakes and be vulnerable. We do the right thing when no one's expecting it. Going from commodity to oddity was a years-long process. The next chapter describes some of the small steps along the way, each growing out of a commitment to treat people right not only inside our company, but also as we do business and present ourselves in the community and larger world.

Chapter Seven Toolbox

IS YOUR BUSINESS A COMMODITY?

The businesses that answer "yes" to the following questions could qualify as a commodity and have an opportunity to position themselves as an oddity.

- Do you have established rivals who compete with you on the basis of price/cost?

- How savvy is your customer base? Can they drive your price down by pitting you and your competitors against one another?

- How powerful is your supplier base? Are they able to constrain your profits by charging you a higher price?

- Can aspiring entrants who are hungry for market share pursue your customers and provide them what you have to offer?

- Are there many substitutes in your market that can lure customers away from using your product or service altogether?

CHAPTER 8

HONOR THY PLUMBER AND THE TRUST SHALL FLOW

Just before New Year's Day a few years ago, I thought, "What if we made a company New Year's resolution? What might that look like? What's something that we can all rally around?" I started thinking about our use of language in the construction industry, which can be crude. But we had already succeeded in cutting out the profanity years earlier. Still, there was one word we all used a lot that was bothering me. What was the dirty word? Subcontractor. I looked up the prefix "sub" in the dictionary, and it said "under, beneath, below."

—MIKE

Our relationship with the skilled tradespeople who do most of the work on our projects and make us successful should not be reflected by a word that implies a "less-than" status. To stop using the word subcontractor, though, would not be easy. We would need a visual reminder, so we came up with a prop. It was a clear twelve-inch plexiglass cube with a hinged, lockable door that opened on top with a slot like you would see on a piggy bank. The first week of January, we put this box in the middle of our main meeting room table. A small sign applied to the front of the box designated it the "Trade Contractor Swear Box."

At the first management meeting of the year, I announced that the company's New Year's resolution was to refer to masons, painters, and other tradespeople as "trade partners" or "trade contractors." I explained my unease at the demeaning term subcontractor. We call ourselves a general contractor, but we are also trade contractors, specializing in shuffling paperwork as we handle the administrative side of the project. Anybody in the company who slipped up and used the term subcontractor would have to put a dollar in the box.

Naturally, some of the team members who had been in the business for decades had a really hard time with the language change. But after a few months, not many dollars were going into the Trade Contractor Swear Box anymore. We left the box in the center of our conference table as a visible reminder of how we honored our trade partners. Our simple resolution became a game changer in our industry as the new terminology took hold with our regional trade association and even among our competitors. Acknowledging and respecting our trade contractors' contributions at the same level as ours was a significant change of thinking.

The prop also became a conversation-starter when we met with new clients. For example, a church building committee came in and saw the words "Swear Box" and thought it was about profanity until we explained the story. About twenty minutes later, John was standing by the whiteboard, explaining the process of awarding contracts, when he said, "This is where we get the bids from the sub-contractors." Before John even finished saying the word, the whole church group rang out like a choir, "John, dollar in the box."

We even heard a story about a lawyer, many times removed from us, giving a speech to a local business group and using the word "sub-contractor." He then stopped himself, corrected it to "trade contractor" and said, "I've got to apologize if there's anybody from Elzinga & Volkers in the audience, because I understand that to be a bad word."

We continue challenging our partners and ourselves to examine how assumptions in our language affect how we do our jobs. We started a new specialty-trade division that involves installing a special fire-stopping caulking material. It is a critical element needed to compartmentalize fires and could save lives in a building such as a hospital. Caulking is not the most complex activity on a construction project, but attention to detail and critical thinking are involved in selecting the right products and installation techniques. We decided to refer to these crew members as "technicians" rather than using the common industry term "installers." That word choice made a big difference in how the crew members approach their job. They seem to take more pride in their appearance and in how they talk about their work. Now we're thinking we'd like to come up with a better term than "laborer" to refer to those who handle menial tasks that, when done well, have a big, positive impact on the job. We believe everyone on the project is critical to its success; everyone's contribution should be honored and appreciated.

OUR EXPERIENCE MANAGER

Another job title that has been important to our company culture is "experience manager." The idea came out of a leadership retreat in which I got some honest feedback about my visionary role. One of the managers said, "We really love your enthusiasm, and we really love all the ideas, but we all have full-time jobs that are quite stressing as they are." To pull off my ideas, the managers said, I needed more help. I didn't have an executive assistant because I didn't think there was enough work to make that a full-time job. But we came up with a broader job description that involved managing how people experience E&V, both inside and outside of our walls.

Morgan, who was promoted to experience manager from inside the company, oversees a year-round calendar of activities, events, and campaigns to deliver an unmistakably E&V experience. It has been made clear that her sole focus is to put a smile on the face of everyone that we touch, and about three-quarters of her work involves the employees. It's not unusual for executives to have an assistant who puts together employee events such as an annual holiday party, but Morgan's job is unique. You'll see in the pages ahead that our activities involve a lot of planning, creativity, and details to show people we care about them as individuals. We strive to avoid "been there, done that" repetition, which puts a lot of pressure on Morgan and her coworkers who pitch in repeatedly to lead and assist in creating and delivering unique experiences.

HOLDING OURSELVES ACCOUNTABLE

In our business, it is important for the outside architects and engineers who work with our projects to be raving fans of our company, too. We were getting raves from our other constituencies. Outside surveys of our employees put us in the Best & Brightest Companies to Work For. Customer satisfaction was showing up in our bottom line, and the trade contractors had twice voted us Michigan Contractor of the

Year. But we were missing feedback from architects. If they voted on awards for contractors, we wondered, what would be their criteria? We didn't know, so we have started to ask them questions such as, "What drives the success of a project? What makes a contractor-architect relationship phenomenal?" We're creating a system to hold ourselves accountable to perform at the highest possible level so that we're the architects' preferred contractor.

Any business could be proactive that way and ask vendors or partner companies, "What if your group gave an award? How would we be judged and how would we rank?" It's a great way to find out what a company needs to work on to make meaningful changes.

Too often companies worry about satisfying their customers but neglect their other business relationships. We mentioned in the previous chapter that our CFO sent a basket of gourmet cookies to our outside accountants to thank them for their hard work helping us get through tax season. The token gift was unmistakably E&V, because while all the big accounting firms' clients pay them significant fees, we were the ones who showed personal gratitude for their work. We're careful to respect ethical rules and limits on gifts clients can take, but we are not constrained by conventional thinking that some professions are necessary evils undeserving of cards or gifts. We say "thank you" to the building inspector, we give our outside auditors a nice space to work and buy them lunch, and we show respect to the guys who empty the porta-jons, recognizing them as a vital part of the job-site success.

TALKING IT OUT

Another way to show respect is to take time to get together and talk through issues. After I joined the Young Presidents Organization as a fledgling CEO, I learned the value of business owners getting together in a room, learning how to be vulnerable, and creating a safe place to have intimate conversations about the good and bad aspects their lives. As part of our efforts to show respect to our trade contractors, we created three similar roundtable groups with them. Each group had about ten people, maybe an electrician, a mechanical contractor, a painter, a concrete contractor, and so on, each representing major trades.

Our approach as the convener was to say, "We're all in the contracting industry. We all have similar challenges and problems. Let's get together on a regular basis and share those." Meetings always begin with a conversation-starter. At the first meeting, the starter was, "Describe a time in your career when you really screwed up." We spoke first to set a level of vulnerability that we expected the others to meet. I shared a story of a million-dollar loss we encountered when starting up a division that just went awry. The idea was, "We all have clay feet. We all have made mistakes," and we could learn by sharing.

It's hard to get busy people together, so we have a disciplined approach to running the meetings and use a timer to stick to the carefully planned agenda. A fun part is going around the table and giving brief updates not just about business but also on personal or family matters. Some items raise issues for further discussion, which we note on a whiteboard. After the updates, we all decide together on two or three items from the issues that had been set aside, or "put in a parking lot" on the whiteboard, to discuss in greater depth. The roundtables have given us a deeper relationship with our trade partners, vis-à-vis our competition or the more traditional contact that occurs through trade-association meetings.

Sample Agenda for Trade Contractor Roundtable

- **Communication starter:** *two to five minutes per person*
- **Personal and professional update:** *five to ten minutes per person*
- **Key topic and discussion** *led by member of the group: thirty to sixty minutes*
- **Parking lot and determine next key topic** *list of future key topics to research: five minutes*
- **Conclusion–rate the meeting:** *five minutes*

A high point of the roundtables was the experience of a founder of a small but fast-growing electrical company. As a high school graduate who became a company president, he confessed he wakes up each day feeling like he doesn't know what to do next, with a fake-it-till-you-make-it mind-set.

"I'll just make it through this day and move on to the next," he said. Many successful people have experienced that feeling, which psychologists call the "imposter syndrome," and the roundtable provided a cure. "Now I finally found a bunch of people whom I can share with and confide in, who will coach me and be my outside board of directors, to create some comfort in how I do business," he said. "This is incredibly powerful."

A left-brained executive might question the business sense of our spending time in these roundtables. We meet about six times a year for no more than three hours so it's not much of a time burden. It was, however, an especially foreign concept in the hierarchical and adversarial construction industry. But, after only a few meetings, we discovered a business-development benefit we didn't anticipate. A trade contractor's leader, who had not known us well in the past, offered to set up a lunch with one of his clients that he thought needed a new general contractor—"Because I think you guys would be a great fit." Likewise, we're much more likely to trust and give work to people we have gotten to know. We've had members of the group come in and share how their spouses were diagnosed with breast cancer. We've cried together in these groups. We've learned to "hold a sacred space" for people to be vulnerable, with no judgment, just support.

A Small Step to Build Trust

In the construction industry, trade contractors who fall behind schedule can expect an angry or threatening phone call from the general contractor's project manager warning them to catch up. Or worse, they may be threatened with removal from the project. Our approach is to have our top leaders meet in person, if possible, with the trade contractor's leadership. "What's going on?" we ask. "What is the real crux of your problem? Be honest with us." Helping them solve their problem rather than beating up on them builds trust, making them more likely to come up with a solution. If your company has been operating in an adversarial way for a long time, it may take that same length of time to build trust, but this kind of meeting is obviously at least a small step forward. They may arrive thinking they are going to be reprimanded and threatened. In our office, quite the opposite occurs when we are empathetic and helpful. We find they are thankful by the time they leave the meeting.

MEASURING TRUST IN RELATIONSHIPS

One way to measure and continuously build trust between colleagues is to use the principles from neuroscience developed by Paul J. Zak, author of the *Trust Factor: The Science of Creating High Performance Companies*. When I met Paul, I found him to be a kindred spirit who used science to arrive at the same truth I discovered through years of work about how powerful trust is in relationships. We both believe that a culture of trust can be developed and is essential to a high-performing company; I see it in smiles and Paul in his use of scientific measures. As the brain responds to social interactions, trust has a neurochemical signal, oxytocin, that can be measured through blood tests.

But we don't have to draw blood to see the business benefits of getting to know our trade contractors as people. When we call for bids, people who know and trust us will quite often give us better prices and put their best people on our jobs. They will reserve time or capacity for us when resources get tight. They will tell us what our competitors are doing wrong and give us honest feedback, both of which help us improve. Our bottom line goes up as the trust factor rises. Projects are more successful because we said, "We need to get these groups of business people together to bear the weight of each other's struggles and to share in each other's successes."

Nonprofit organizations may have similar issues. They see each other as competitors if they are chasing after the same donors and sponsors. But they also may have separate, complementary missions, such as providing food, shelter, and education. Their executive directors could come together in roundtables and ask, "Can we help each other out with how we go about raising money, how we hire and train people, and how we engage and honor volunteers?"

Exposing vulnerability and breaking down walls can be especially valuable in any industry that is transactional and cost-driven. It's counterintuitive if you are in a cutthroat business, but being open about your challenges can lead to unexpected solutions or advances in the way you do business. Breaking down traditional barriers doesn't always work, but we've found it works a lot of the time. It may turn out that the walls were there only because they always had been there—not because they were load-bearing.

Our trade contractors also benefit from our leadership in developing a safety program we have called Alive365®. The idea began in 2013 when we were approaching a major safety milestone, 2,500 days without a lost-time accident. "We should have a big celebration. We'll invite our trade partners," we thought. Tony, our chief operating officer, suggested a symposium with speakers to not just celebrate but also remind ourselves of the importance of safety. To make the event unmistakably E&V, we let it grow into a weeklong affair in which we hired experts in multiple locations throughout our region to train our trade partners' people at our expense on various safety protocols such as first aid, aerial lifts, and fall protection. We realized that trade partners can't justify the expense of hiring an expert to train a few people, but we could justify the cost and the time by spreading the benefit so widely. We also felt a moral obligation, because as the Bible teaches, we are our brothers' keepers.

We have made the Alive365® training an annual event as a way of giving back to the people who make us successful—our trade partners. It costs about $50,000 a year and has reached as many as two thousand people over four years. Some were surprised that we took on a safety expense for others, but we want them to feel we are a very special firm to work with. Again, an idea that started out with our trying to do the right thing has become a competitive advantage. This unmistakably different program was likely a major reason why we received the top national award out of twenty-one thousand members of our trade association.

Alive 365® by the numbers

	Totals
Companies	2/6
People	1314
Trainings	46

We began this chapter describing how we used "trade contractor" to get away from a demeaning term. Giving a position a lower status may make it easier to discharge someone who is not doing a good job, but we have found that showing respect for people creates a better dynamic not only with employees and customers but also in all business relationships. We have seen deepening relationships with business partners pay off over the years in our bottom line and in our company reputation. The logical next step in our journey was to share our approach with others in our community and industry. The next chapter shows how we take our philosophy beyond our own business.

Chapter Eight Toolbox

CASE FOR THIRD PARTY EVALUATION

The Best and Brightest Companies to Work For is an organization that holds a nationwide competition to rank organizations on a wide variety of factors that contribute to employee satisfaction and engagement. By using an outside resource and programming like the Best and Brightest program, your employees can trust that their responses will be kept confidential, allowing them to respond honestly. The gathered data is compared to other companies in your region and across the nation.

We have participated in this program for over ten years, earning top honors regionally and nationally. We take the information shared with us from the Best and Brightest and use it to develop internal programming through ten employee-led committees whose mission is to keep improving one area of the company. For instance, in one of our first surveys we learned that we weren't communicating as well as other organizations in our region, even though our leadership team thought we were strong in this area. We took a serious look at how and when we were communicating and adapted some of the new tools and delivery methods. This resulted in a 28 percent improvement in our communication score the next year. Without this third-party feedback, our leadership team would have continued thinking that we were communicating well, missing a great opportunity for improvement.

While employee engagement surveys aren't a new concept, the value of third-party administration and benchmarking has proven to be tremendously valuable to our company. The ability to compare ourselves to our peers keeps us on our toes and fuels a healthy level of competition. It allows us to use data to drive decision making and programming versus relying on intuition, and we have an indicator telling us if a new program was successful or not. And, on top of it all, we have been able to fill our trophy case along the way, giving our team a reason to celebrate and a means to validate our employee-centric culture.

CHAPTER 9

USING ALL HANDS AND TULIPS TO SPREAD THE WORD

Three times a year our local diocese holds an event called the Catholic Business Leaders Forum. I was invited to speak to the gathering of about two hundred business leaders on how I draw on my Christian morals and Roman Catholic faith at work. I talked about the right-brained approaches that have been explained in this book. Speaking about those "What Would Jesus Do?" bracelets some Christians wear, I half-jokingly suggested that Jesus was a right-brained leader. I don't think anybody disputed my statement, since Jesus brought compassion, generosity, spirituality, and creativity to teaching His disciples. Jesus told wonderfully relatable parables. He didn't spend left-brained time telling his disciples how many people to preach the faith to per day or draw a hockey-stick-shaped image in the sand to convey His three-year conversion plan. If we want to embody leadership that has been honored for more than two thousand years, I said, why not try to do so from a Christian perspective?

—**MIKE**

Our community business leaders were receptive to a message that they could be held in high regard for doing right-brain-driven things that you can't see or touch. It's kind of a blind faith that you will do well in business by doing right.

Jesus exemplifies servant leadership—leading from behind, love in teaching, resolving conflict rather than creating more conflict, all concepts that inspire the philosophy we have discussed in this book. We believe strongly that you can apply this approach to any business, and if you are so inclined you can use the way Jesus lived as an example for your business. We base our business on Christ's teachings but respect those who may not be so comfortable with overt expressions of personal Christian values in a business setting.

AWARDS PROVIDE VALIDATION AND MORE

A subject that comes up more often when we speak in public is the number of awards our company has won. In fact, you may be asking, "How much time does that company spend entering contests?" Unapologetically, we spend a lot of time entering contests. One reason is that prospective customers don't have to just take our word that we're the best; we have validation from outside parties. Just as important, entering contests helps us be introspective and focus on our performance in the criteria being judged. Winning awards is great for morale, but the awards are also a driver for us to constantly improve. We like entering the Best and Brightest Companies to Work For contest because winning that award shines a light on the good things we're doing for our people. Winning Michigan Contractor of the Year helps us spread the message in our industry that things like our culture of safety-first and respectful treatment of trade partners lead to success.

We've made changes that give us a competitive advantage, and we're showing that to our industry, pushing the entire industry to change. If that happens, competition will be on a more level playing field, but we're okay with everybody operating at a high level.

We also try to inspire our employees to be award-worthy in their family and personal lives. We want them to be thought of as the Neighbor of the Year because they do little things like take the neighbor's garbage cans in from the curb. Spreading our workplace philosophy throughout our lives can be very powerful outside of business.

Mike Talks about His Personal Brand

When we introduce new hires to the unmistakable E&V brand we mention that it can be taken outside the workplace and extended as a personal brand. Here's how I give a personal example of how one might build a "Husband of the Year" brand: I could be the guy who comes home, hangs up my coat, and settles into the easy chair with my newspaper and favorite beverage because I've worked hard, had a stressful day, and need time for myself. Or I can come home, converse with my wife, play with my kids, and help prepare dinner. That's a whole different experience of a husband and father being present.

For any man to be worthy of a Husband of the Year Award, he must act differently than most husbands do.

Even ordinary things can be done in a proactive and unmistakable way. For example, when the kids go to bed, my wife and I might sit down over tea and talk for a half-hour or so about our day and just enjoy each other's company. I buy a Hallmark card, write something really loving in it, and may put it on her pillow at night, by the sink where she gets ready in the morning, or send it by good old-fashioned snail mail in my signature yellow envelope so she immediately knows it's from me and is excited to open it. This happens not just on her birthday, not just on Valentine's Day, and not just on our anniversary, but on any day I've chosen to make special—because she's special in my life.

TULIPS AND GIANT WOODEN SHOES

In projecting our company culture outward into our community, we have drawn on the Dutch heritage of our founders, Elzinga & Volkers, and our location, Holland, Michigan. The city hosts Tulip Time, the largest Dutch-heritage festival in the US, drawing hundreds of thousands of visitors. A lot of the visitors pass right by our offices in the heart of the city. Like almost everyone else in town, we have planted tulips that are blooming in May during the festival. We got used to seeing festivalgoers sitting on curbs, using our beautiful tulips as a photo backdrop. So, we constructed a better backdrop—a billboard-sized old-fashioned "Welcome to Holland" postcard with the festival name and date and a windmill-filled image of the Netherlands. We placed antique-looking wooden planters full of tulips where they would appear in any photos taken in front of the giant postcard.

The idea was to show corporate pride in our community, the same reason our company has a float each year in the city's annual Christmas Parade of Lights. Tulip Time also has parades, and we decided they needed a special float. We got an idea from some wooden-shoe knickknacks we had sitting in our office. Our steel, carpentry, and finishing shops worked together to build twelve-foot-long "wooden shoes" and mounted them on new zero-turn garden tractors. We began with a steel whalebone sub frame, applied bent wood like on a ship, then plastered and finally covered with a layer of fiberglass to make them weatherproof. We painted on faux woodgrain so they looked as if they were carved from giant blocks of wood. The wow factor was huge. This showcasing of our craftsmanship received tremendous attention in the media—and, yes, we won a best-float award. It recognized our success doing something important in our right-brained company culture, memorably bringing smiles to people's faces.

As a fundraiser for Tulip Time 2017, we corralled the wooden shoes and postcard scene in our parking lot and took donations from those who availed themselves of the photo opportunity. In subsequent years, we hope our idea takes off and other businesses create their own fund-raising photo ops.

FUN WAYS TO GIVE TO CHARITY

A lot of companies have community initiatives such as charity drives in which you can see the left-brained influence. They have calculated that a socially responsible image will appeal to customers or help with recruiting. Our approach is to use charitable activities as an opportunity to connect our people internally and with their community. For example, we had a team-building exercise in which groups of employees each visited a local nonprofit to learn about their respective missions and work. The teams returned to the office and pitched "their" nonprofit to a panel of judges, in the style of the television show, *Shark Tank*. The judges then granted money to the most deserving charities. That was a creative, right-brained way to make writing checks to charities, which a lot of business leaders do, into a training opportunity for our people in making team presentations. At the same time, our people directly interacted with the nonprofits. They felt the joy of giving and could brag to their friends and family how they got paid to give away money at work.

Mike Describes a Commitment to Hurricane Relief

I sit on the board of the group that puts on the Best and Brightest Companies to Work For competition. After Hurricane Harvey devastated Houston in 2017, my connection to that national group led to a request to help provide disaster relief. We donated a lot of time working in Michigan to find resources for rebuilding Houston. It was the right thing to do, even though we were a thousand miles away and had a lot of important issues in our own backyard.

We have two more fun variations in our charitable giving. One involves a pro-football championship office pool. We place the bets in the names of nonprofits. In 2018, the game popularly known as "Super Bowl squares" benefited organizations focused on construction-workforce development. We could have just written a check, but this way, the employees and beneficiaries got to share in the excitement as they watched the big game on TV. The previous year, twenty nonprofits with five squares each ended up sharing these sheets with their staff and boards so hundreds of people we didn't know became aware of us in a fun and exciting way.

Another unusual way we give away money involves the Geo-caching treasure hunt app. In this online game, strangers can get clues to find "treasures" that people hide. We were planning to make a generous gift to a nonprofit client's capital campaign, but rather than just mailing back the pledge card, we sent coordinates to find our pledge. They'd have to search the latitude and longitude using some type of GPS device. That challenge was a stretch for the non-profit's development officers, but they had some tech-savvy young people in the organization get into a car with them for what turned out to be a fun field trip into the woods. The game included hints that provided a code to open a locked metal box hidden in leaves on a hilltop.

How do you judge the generosity of a charity pledge? Left-brained thinking would look at the amount. So, for our left brained readers, we regularly give more than 10 percent of our net income to nonprofits and charitable organizations. But our right-brained approach offers something more—a memorable experience for both our people who set up the treasure hunt and the nonprofit's people who participate. Many businesses are generous and give back to their community, but if they don't engage the right brain they miss an opportunity to create unique experiences and fond memories. Just as a bonus check is less memorable to employees than a special personal-ized gift, electronically moving money into a nonprofit's general fund doesn't leave its people feeling connected with your people through a shared experience.

SHOWING GRATITUDE IS REWARDING

We apply the same approach with other interactions outside of our organization. For example, our industry has to deal with building inspectors. They can make trouble for a contractor, so it tends to be an adversarial relationship. We know building inspectors have a job to do, enforcing codes in everyone's best interests, so we treat building inspectors as just another part of the team. We'll often send them a thank-you letter acknowledging their part in creating a successful project, and maybe copy in their boss. That's unheard of for a profession used to only getting complaints.

Having our company culture go beyond our office walls—whether in a letter, a giant postcard, or a parade float—is something we consider a success. We give speeches to spread the word about the value of our business philosophy. Inevitably the audience includes left-brained thinkers who ask about the bottom line. We estimate that for every dollar we invest in our company culture, we get $5 in return. Since the end of the Great Recession, our top-line revenue has stayed fairly consistent with some growth, but our profits have grown three to four times as much as our revenue. There are many reasons, summarized below.

Within our enterprise ...

- we practically eliminated costly personnel turnover.

- recruiting got much easier, with most hiring resulting from in-house referrals or an exodus from competing contractors with broken cultures.

- our employees became more productive because they were happy in their jobs, trusted their leaders, understood their connection to the corporate mission, and maintained a healthy work/life balance. (Five more productive hours, not additional hours, a week from a salaried employee is a 12.5 percent increase in productivity.)

- employees learned to "self-regulate" and correct each other's behavior, saving executives time spent enforcing rules.

- employees feel connected to the organization and part of a team acting as an extension of our CEO, looking out for the reputation, health, and profitability of the organization. In effect, all our people serve in a corporate-leadership role throughout the course of their workday.

And on the client side ...

- we didn't really need a sales department because clients sought us out.

- we could ask for a better-than-average return on projects when we were the clear favorite general contractor.

- clients became willing to pay for added value as they came to understand that we are unmistakably different in how we perform our jobs and create a unique energy on their project with their staff.

- we could avoid undesirable projects that were going to be given to the lowest bidder regardless of value.

Being hired for a project when we are among the higher bidders is proof of concept for our skeptics, and gives us great joy because it allows us to treat our people even better and to do even more for them. When our employees love what they do and love who they work alongside, they are more productive, which lowers overhead. The resulting improved profitability then funds more things the company can do to show its care for its team members.

If a company wants to gauge whether it is offering a great place to work, it could just ask the employees' children. They notice whether their parents come home from work excited and happy or not. We have employees who say their kids want to work for E&V, in a region with lots of job opportunities.

We have employees who brag so much about their place of work that neighbors ask, "Are they hiring?" When we are talking with potential new hires, we don't hesitate to give them our employee roster, so they can call anyone on it to ask how it is to work at E&V.

Mike Recalls a Visit from a Skeptic

I was in my office chatting with a business owner who was not convinced our philosophy could work. His left-brained reaction to my stories was that we seemed to be playing around all day and couldn't be getting much work done.

"How do you know people appreciate or even notice all these things you do?" he asked. I got up from my desk and walked across the room to my credenza, slid open a file drawer, and pulled out a bulging folder. It was about four inches thick, full of thank-you cards and letters of appreciation from business associates, employees, and their family members. And there are just as many plaudits stored as emails. I cherish them all as validation that people like the way we do business.

Human capital is a great resource that many organizations complain they have trouble attracting. We have our employees telling their children, friends, and people they meet in the field that E&V is a great place to work. A business theory holds that if an employee is making $20 an hour at Company X, the "poaching premium" is the amount of additional wages Company Y would have to pay to lure that employee. Pay is only one of many reasons people change jobs, but it is part of the equation. An employee who hates Company X might jump to Company Y for $18 an hour, a negative premium. An indifferent employee might move for $20.50 an hour. What if an employee loves Company X, has many friends there, and his or her family members are raving fans of the company? It might cost Company Y $30 or maybe even $40 an hour to poach that employee. If an organization's employees are jumping ship for the same money, culture's probably an issue.

Our CFO, Grace, was recently at an industry meeting, talking with an executive who liked his job but was considering moving for a nice bump in pay. As she recounted the story, she said, "I told the guy that somebody could offer me double what I'm making right now, and I wouldn't leave. It wouldn't be worth it." That statement reflects a culture of trust that an employer is not going to abuse an employee for being honest and loyal. Having an employee acknowledge that pay is far down the scale of what makes a job valuable is a measure that we're getting a great return on investment for the other things we do for our employees.

Another leader within our company told us she came aboard for the same salary she was previously earning even though the change added ninety minutes of commuting time to her day.

As our company has grown, we've had an influx of young female professionals joining us around the time they're getting married and starting families. In a traditionally male-dominated construction company, having just a few pregnant women seemed like a baby boom. In our right-brained thinking, the baby boom was another positive sign of success. People who enjoy their jobs and feel they have a clear mission for which they receive training and acknowledgment at work will go home feeling joyful. They will not only be a more engaged husband, wife, father, or mother, but their positive mood tends to play out physically as well. How many people feel like making love when they've had a miserable day at work?

A company culture resonates beyond the walls of the organization that creates it. In this chapter we have shared stories that we hope challenge you to look at everything you do in your organization and personal life and find an unmistakable way to do it, a way that will create fond memories for those you touch. Participating in community affairs, giving away money, and being socially responsible can be approached in creative ways that connect with employees and help them learn and build their personal brand in every relationship they have. Below we have a few tips to get started, and in the final chapter we offer examples and exercises to inspire your journey to becoming unmistakable.

Sending a Hidden Message

When we renovated our break room, we needed to replace a stair railing. We asked our steel-fabricating shop to be creative in the design. People might not notice until we point it out, but the steel is welded together in such a way that it forms smiley faces along the way up the railing. It has an S at the bottom, which stands for "start here," and the smiles lead up to a dollar sign at the top, reflecting our belief that if we see smiles on the faces of our clients and employees, profits will follow. It's another way for us to tell newcomers and visitors our story and reinforce the ideas of creativity, innovation, and right-brained thinking.

Chapter Nine Toolbox

NEXT STEPS TO START THE JOURNEY

Start small by saying, "thank you," and really meaning it!

- Many leaders, whether they're at work or at home, can fall into the trap of over using "thank you" to the point where it loses its meaning. Gratitude needs to be genuine and meaningful to have the desired impact on culture and company performance. Consider these steps next time you write a thank you note or give someone verbal thanks:

  - Be specific about what you are thanking a person for.

    "Bill, thank you for turning in that report a day early."

- Share how you were impacted by the person's actions.

  "I was able to respond to our client faster because of your efforts."

- Try to connect positive behavior to your corporate values.

  "Responding early to our clients requests is a great way to be unmistakable. Great work."

Hold your first leadership retreat.

- We have shared multiple stories from our leadership retreats and specifics on how to make those retreats meaningful. Now it is time to schedule one. Give ample notice to your leadership teams and make sure that all your key leaders are available. Keep some specifics of the retreat secret to build anticipation. Your retreats should be something that employees should be looking forward to, not dreading.

Start sharing the positive.

- We told you that Elzinga & Volkers holds weekly meetings to "savor our successes" and focus on the positive aspects of our business and personal lives. A weekly meeting may not work for everyone, but the concept of publicly sharing positive news is key to having a happy, engaged workforce that will strive to be unmistakable.

Consider a video blog series where employees can highlight good news from their area of the company. Consider a program where employees are encouraged to send gratitude notes to each other. Talk with your leaders about consciously sharing more good news with employees than bad, even when working through challenging issues.

The ultimate goal is to hard wire a real sense of positivity in your team. A genuine sense that there is a bright side to any situation will start to change your team's perspective and expose solutions and opportunities that may have been hidden from your organization.

Leverage outside resources.

- Do not be afraid to ask for help from peer groups, outside consultants, and your family. When you set out on this journey, you will need ideas and inspiration from outside of your walls to succeed. It is well documented that new, industry-changing ideas typically come from outside of an organization, not from groups only focused inward. Fill your mental "basket" with new information and ideas not only to inspire, but to also avoid the mistakes of others.

CHAPTER 10

LET THE MAGIC BEGIN

How exactly do you engage your right brain? It takes exercise, and we'll begin with a technique we learned about in the book Thinkertoys.

—MIKE

An exercise called the lotus blossom is a grid that you can fill out on a big poster board. If the grid is nine-by-nine, there are eighty-one squares, and you start by placing your theme in the center square. Suppose you enter a goal there, "Buy a new home." If you are setting out on such a major endeavor, you are going to have a lot of thoughts scrambled in your head. Organizing them on the grid helps you visualize how they connect to each other.

You fill in the eight squares that surround the center square with your main considerations for buying a new home, such as location, size, price, and amenities. Then you build around each of those eight squares with the various possibilities you can envision for location, size, and so on. By the time you have filled in eighty-one squares, you can see many factors in perspective. It's a more graphical way of seeing the looming decisions, compared with a more traditional left-brained approach of making a list or outline. If you make an outline, and location is number one, then you might just write, "Number one, location: (a) city, (b) suburb," and then go onto, "Number two, size: (a) three bedrooms, (b) four bedrooms." Having six more boxes to fill in forces you to think creatively about other real possibilities for yourself, because you don't want to leave boxes blank. Next thing you know maybe you have decided to buy an RV and live as a nomad, start a commune, live on a cruise ship, or more likely stay put and remodel.

LOTUS BLOSSOM

			amenities				
			amenities			three car garage	
	location	location	buy a new home	size	size		two baths
			price			three bedrooms	
			price				

We have used the lotus blossom exercise in management meetings to challenge each other to come up with ways to grow our business and become unmistakable. We find that having a visual representation of all the possibilities gets everyone excited. *Thinkertoys*, a book by Michael Michalko, an expert on creative thinking techniques, deserves a lot of credit for deepening our creative thinking. We've shown some of the exercises to clients and nonprofit boards that later also adopted them.

Creativity involves a lot more than brainstorming goals in a conference room; it also comes into play in the care and feeding of personal relationships. We spend a lot of time thinking creatively about how to reward our team's best players. A minimal way to personalize a gift is to put a handwritten note into the envelope with a bonus check. Sometimes a well-chosen, non-monetary gift means a lot more to people. A cash reward can be a cold experience without much staying power, especially at companies that announce annual bonuses via a mass email and dispense them by direct deposit.

We celebrate major milestones in a big way. When our executive committee closed the deal to buy our privately held company, we decided to really celebrate by taking the key people who pulled off the deal on a trip with spouses to Las Vegas. The trip was filled with surprises, including being picked up by a limousine, shows, dinners, a trip to Hoover Dam, and picking out a personalized gift. We created a memorable group experience with the gift as a lasting reminder.

You might wonder how a big organization can personalize gifts; it's hard enough for the CEO to know everybody's name as an organization gets bigger. In the paperwork our new employees fill out, we have a unique form that asks people to list a few favorite things: favorite animal, color, candy, movie, vacation, and so on. They forget they filled out this frivolous form, but we keep it on file. Then, for example, a few years later at a company Christmas party they are given an individual gift bag with items that seem to have been picked out by a mind reader. Each employee gets his or her favorite candy, except the guy who wrote on his form, "I don't like candy. I would prefer to eat green beans." His bag contains a can of green beans.

Knowing our employees' families also helps us personalize gifts. That's how we found just the right guitar to give to one of our field managers at his retirement party. His wife knew that guitar would be something he would cherish for the rest of his life.

Imagine going to a meeting and being seated at a place that has not only your name on a tent card but your usual choice of coffee, tea, or soft drink. Or perhaps you received a questionnaire before the meeting that inexplicably asked about your favorite childhood snack, and there it is at your seat. You start the meeting smiling over a good childhood memory rather than ruminating over some recent email. These personalization gestures change your perception of how you fit into the organization. Similarly, we can create a communal feeling at a retreat by renting a large cottage and cooking together rather than using a hotel and restaurants. Reliance on each other and shared experiences elevates the way we can do business when we return to the office.

The outcome can be especially amazing when someone on the team is under duress. We celebrated with our project administrator, Tara, when she came back from maternity leave after having her first child. But a month later, she found out that her son, Nolan, had a serious illness that required lengthy treatment. We have family-leave benefits, but our employees approached us unprompted and asked us if they could donate vacation days to extend Tara's paid leave to make it easier for her to spend more time with Nolan. The response was overwhelming, resulting in a total of seventy-seven days of vacation time given, including a whole week from one employee. That creative solution shows how behavior we have modeled for our employees had become so ingrained that they reacted to a crisis in an unmistakable way.

We have engaged in a lot of team-building activities that you may be able to borrow or adapt for your organization. Like a lot of companies, we have summer outings and management retreats, but we try to make them unusually fun and different each time. If the employees planning an event suggest something too familiar, we push back and ask, "How are we making this unmistakable?" We push the team to be creative, and don't take that burden entirely on ourselves.

Geocaching scavenger hunt: In the last chapter we told the story of a treasure hunt we created for a nonprofit beneficiary of our charitable giving. We did something similar for our office staff, breaking into five groups of six people for a scavenger hunt using the Geocaching app. First, they found a mini safe with a combination lock and a note directing them to a vehicle. Then they got directions to find a riddle to crack the safe. Inside the safe was a $200 gift card to Subway, where they were instructed to buy themselves lunch and use the balance of the card to buy lunch for the next people who came through the restaurant door. We told them to take pictures and get reactions.

There were more stops, including one where we instructed them to re-enact a historical event and send us a picture. At the last stop, they ended up in the woods following seventy-five yards of string to a hidden foam cooler full of celebratory drinks. We followed up with a pizza party at headquarters where we could share all their stories and photos. It was a fantastic way to energize our staff and well worth the planning it took by three of us who stayed back at base camp directing the action.

The stakeholders meeting: We have a small number of shareholders in our closely held company. So instead of an annual shareholder meeting, we invite everybody who gets a paycheck from the company to an annual stakeholder meeting. They hear reports and financial details similar to what shareholders would hear. When we first tried this, it was an eye-opener to how much our people longed to know the details about where we've been and where we're going as a company.

We share information about upcoming initiatives and what employees can expect to see in the coming one-to-three years. We find that by communicating our "corporate plans" to the entire population, everybody is more engaged in contributing to make the plans come to fruition. Communicating the bigger picture to everybody in the company helps bridge the disconnection between people of different departments and "ranks." When employees are later asked for some information or to do something out of the ordinary, they have context for the request and are happy and proud to contribute.

Savoring-Our-Successes Meeting: Inviting everyone who is available to attend a meeting every Friday morning provided an early opportunity for us to set a tone of open sharing in which we insist on knowing each other. The first part of the Savoring-Our-Successes Meeting offers employees a chance to talk about joyful things happening in their personal lives, like running their first 5k or having their child graduate from high school. The second part is about business successes such as finishing a project. Previously we had just been going from one project to the next without ever stopping to enjoy the moment of success.

Our Savoring-Our-Successes Meeting started during the Great Recession when people were having a hard time staying happy and motivated and feeling grateful. As this book goes to press, we have done it weekly for almost a decade, and it has created great energy and feelings of being connected. We also have mounted a magnet board in our break room where we share photos or artifacts related to the success stories. The board is divided into quarters, signifying the four quarters in a year. We leave the "evidence" of the success or happy memory up for an entire year. This way, each time our team members pass through this area, they are reminded of the joys that we've shared.

Meeting starters: If an organization is just starting to develop a culture of trust, it helps to begin a meeting by saying, "Share with the group one thing about yourself that probably nobody knows," and then go around the room. It's also important that the leader shares first to set the level of vulnerability and intimacy that is appropriate. If you say, "When I was thirteen years old, my brother got hit by a car and killed," that might be too much for an initial trust-building meeting. But if you say something like, "When I was thirty years old, I went skydiving with all my groomsmen before I got married," that would be more appropriate, memorable, and personal than just sharing your favorite color. Our company has developed a fair amount of trust and intimacy. In one of our group meetings, a woman who worked for us for about three years announced to the room, "Three years to this date, I was pronounced fully in remission from cancer." Nobody at our company knew that about her past.

No vending machines: To promote our culture of sharing, we needed to create a physical space that our employees enjoy being in. During a headquarters renovation, we turned our boardroom into more of a community meeting room. We did a ribbon cutting, put out sodas and big bowls of snacks, and invited all the employees in. They were enjoying a space constructed by their coworkers, and somebody said, "Oh, wouldn't it be so cool if we had these amenities every day?" We ended up removing the vending machines from the break room and keeping the meeting room refrigerator full of juices, soda, and water, along with three big jars full of peanut M&Ms, mixed nuts, and peanut butter-filled pretzels. The annual cost is around two thousand dollars. The payoff is that we see smiles on the faces of employees' kids when they are brought in to see their parent's workplace. And we know the amenity is a factor in our regularly winning best-workplace awards.

Christmas party video: We create a video for our Christmas party each year, and it typically involves the executive team making fun of ourselves, such as by dressing up in funny costumes. When leadership is seen as human, it enhances team building. The videos weave in the successes we've experienced that year in a lighthearted way. Each year, our employees will be talking about the video for weeks afterward and re-watching it to see if they missed anything or just for laughs.

Paintball and mud runs: Entry-level staff, some as young as eighteen, can be nervous around the top executives. If the CEO comes to an outing and plays paintball with them, it puts them on an equal playing field for a while. Shooting the CEO with a paintball or competing together in a mud run is the kind of memory that sticks with people. Organizations that don't have the resources to plan their own team-building outings can participate together in outside experiential events such as a Warrior Dash, Spartan Race, or whatever comes to their community.

The benefits of leaders showing vulnerability are immeasurable. When you come back on Monday morning and your people have seen you crawl through the mud, or a junior staff member has helped you crawl under barbed wire, they are more likely to come in and bring you an idea or suggestion. They share their knowledge from the field. They know you as a person, they know you care about them, and they don't want to let you down.

Mike Recalls When the Trophy Case Was Empty

We were working on a renovation at a hospital that wanted to get rid of a glass trophy case that was about six feet high and two feet wide. Our project manager asked me, "Do we want this? Do we have anything to put in it?" I decided to have him bring it to our lobby. The challenge of filling that empty trophy case was the genesis of our culture of trying to act award-worthy. The visual of an empty trophy case sitting in our lobby helped change the way we do business. It's overflowing now, and we have trophies and awards on nearby tables and in various other rooms.

One of our biggest innovations in support of our company culture came from the realization that all employees need some flexibility to fulfill personal obligations that are important to them. As the CEO, I had the freedom to take time off to drive each of my twins, a son and a daughter, to college at the beginning of their freshman year. Helping them move into two different campuses two weeks apart was emotional and important. We decided to help make sure our people don't miss their son's or daughter's soccer championship or recital because they happen during work hours. We call the program a Hall Pass, because unlike vacation or personal days, it provides eight hours of paid time off that can be broken up throughout the year, as they need it. Employees requesting a Hall Pass must share what it is they're going to do and submit a picture with their family member showing the circumstance that they signed up for.

While our construction guys might use their vacation to go hunting, drawing them further away from family, the Hall Pass ensures they get more involved in their family lives. With two hundred employees, it was a big deal for us to give up what could amount to 1,600 hours of staff time. But it has been outweighed by the appreciation shown by the employees and their willingness to work harder on other days.

We've talked a lot about fun things we do, so it's important to note that making time for those activities requires disciplined time management. We may start a meeting with a playful, personal starter question but we still follow a strict agenda. We use the proven Entrepreneurial Operating System advocated by Gino Wickman in his book, *Traction*. One component, the L10 meeting format, calls for going around the room at the end of a meeting to ask everybody to rank how well the time was spent. We aim for the highest rating, level 10. We flip the switch to our left brain to make sure we are getting our work done, even if our goal is to get that work out of the way to make time for more camaraderie and creativity.

Whatever tools and systems you use, the magic begins at the very top with a leader who understands that strong, deep, and productive relationships require a level of intimacy to build trust. You can be that leader by engaging your right brain, treating everyone well, showing vulnerability, and fostering creativity in the workplace in ways such as the ones we covered in this chapter. We'll close our case with a few final words in the Conclusion.

Chapter Ten Toolbox

TAKE OFF YOUR ARMOR TO WIN THE BATTLE

Now that you've read a few techniques for creating trust within your team, reflect on how you show up at work and what tone you're setting for vulnerability. A few questions to consider:

- Do your coworkers know your spouse's name?
- Do they know where you live?
- Do you engage with your coworkers when you see them outside of the office?

- Do your coworkers know something about you from when you were in college?
- Can you be self-deprecating in front of your team?
- Have you shared your biggest failure in business?
- Do your coworkers know how you recharge?
- Have you shared what makes you happiest? What about what you think makes for a great day at work?
- Does your team know your biggest current pressure?
- Do you share information about your passions outside of work?
- Do your teammates know what you respect them for and vice versa?
- Have you openly shared how you define success?
- Would you invite any of your team members to a major life event (wedding, milestone birthday party, etc.)?

If you answer "no" to most of these questions, you probably aren't being very open with your team and, as the leader, you set the tone. Consider using some of the techniques mentioned earlier in this book, or looking for other ways you can create openness and comfort in being vulnerable with your team. Start with something small and see how your team receives you, or consider talking with a colleague who will give you honest feedback.

CONCLUSION

BECOMING UNMISTAKABLE

We have recounted our journey from commodity to oddity spanning over more than a decade. Readers who are just coming into a business, or leaders who are just starting to think about a cultural transformation, may find it a stretch to share and be vulnerable and generous in the ways we have described. But the starting point can be as easy as admitting when you've made a mistake or admitting that you fear embarking on this journey. You can begin simply by publicly telling people how valuable they are.

Right-brained leadership. Leadership from the heart. Living the Golden Rule. Call it what you want, but focusing on and caring about the people with whom you work is simply the right thing to do. It's how we all want to be treated, and when we are, we stick with those relationships. Whether it's a relationship with a family member, friend, coworker, customer, supplier, or competitor, the philosophy just works. And it will return your investment, however it is measured, tenfold. Our experience has proven this.

The most valuable asset in any business is *people*. People who are engaged and happy in their work perform better than those who are not. Those who feel treasured and trusted to use their talents and judgment will embrace being a part of something larger than themselves. They will think and act like owners. They will pick up and take out the trash when nobody is looking. They won't even return calls from your competitors' recruiters.

The battle for talent is among the biggest challenges for businesses and nonprofit organizations, especially in a tight employment market. The cost of turnover is extremely high, particularly for key employees. At times, skilled labor simply isn't available for growing businesses. For service-based companies where staff talent and client relationships represent the only business assets, the stakes are even higher. Ask yourself, "Can I afford to not invest in my most important assets?"

The investment starts at the top of an organization with a simple willingness to be vulnerable and a structure that will support a people-centric vision. It requires sincerity—a sincere vision for how you approach your employees and all aspects of the value chain supporting your business. If you don't mean it, don't attempt it. If you do, this book provides tangible tools to start investing in the relationships that drive your business.

Some businesses have no choice but to charge the lowest price, but that imperative does not mean that the techniques in this book can't help them by reducing cost and increasing productivity and retention. The companies that we think can benefit the most are the ones that blame all their troubles on external factors while putting no effort into the internal culture of their organization.

Remember, we haven't abandoned use of the left brain. We are committed to a disciplined approach to business. We apply analytical tools to identify business drivers, engage in intensive planning processes, and execute with accountability. Our track record demonstrates strong financial performance, and we believe in making money. But when that discipline is combined with a right-brained management philosophy, something truly powerful happens. With support from your employees, supplier partners, customers, and communities, your business can scale faster and more sustainably. Most important, you will bring more joy to the lives of everyone you touch.

We opened this book with a reference to *The Wizard of Oz*. In one of the movie's last scenes, Dorothy goes around saying her goodbyes to the characters. She embraces the Scarecrow and says, "I think I'm going to miss you most of all." We know that feeling, because we have created a workplace so caring and meaningful that people hate to leave.

In a business setting, sadly there are some people who won't understand and embrace the cultural change you are making and will be lost along the way. They want to have a traditional employer-employee relationship and won't fit into an oddity company. That's the biggest challenge of an otherwise fulfilling and joyful journey.

Leaders who create the right atmosphere, not only chasing after money, but, instead, keeping top of mind the people we deal with, will build an unmistakably different organizational culture. It will be rewarding in every way.

WOULD YOU LIKE OUR HELP STARTING YOUR JOURNEY TO BECOMING UNMISTAKABLE?

Visit us at **www.BecomeUnmistakable.com** and we would love to help.

Led by a team of business professionals who have taken their organizations from the black and white world of business as usual into the colorful world of business like no other, **Become Unmistakable™** is passionate about infusing companies with employee-centric disciplines and right-brained leadership to reduce turnover, increase engagement, and make you unmistakable in your market.

Become Unmistakable™ offers flexible training and con-sulting opportunities along with ongoing support to leaders who strive to be something unique. No matter the industry, if people are your biggest asset and the source of your strongest competitive advantage, the journey to Become Unmistakable is for you.

PRAISE FOR MIKE, JOHN, AND
BECOME UNMISTAKABLE

Mike and John have unmistakably defined what it means to enjoy what you do, who you do it with, and why you do it in the first place. Their commitment, passion, and ability to achieve business excellence has set the bar at a new height for anyone who wishes to be the best at what they do and do it with teamwork, fun, and style!

SETH WEHNER
President, SWMGT

From the moment you meet the leadership team and the rest of the staff, you know there is something special about E&V. Three things seem to standout and make them so unique: a creative and supportive work culture, family focused initiatives, and safety [above] all. They are so focused and enthused about these values that you almost forget they are a construction company!

MARK MORROW
Consultant, The Breton Group

I've have had the pleasure of knowing Mike Novakoski for the last fifteen years. On a professional basis, I have been so impressed for what he has accomplished at Elzinga & Volkers. As a business person myself, it is very obvious to me that it is Mike's leadership abilities and fundamental beliefs that have allowed E&V to grow into the fabulous company it is today. Working hard, being honest and transparent, [and] treating employees as valued individuals while honoring and serving his customers are hallmarks of his core philosophy and subsequent actions. He simply does things the right way.

On a personal level, I admire the way Mike lives out this portion of his life as well. While he works diligently and has built a successful company, he has never lost sight of his priorities, which are his faith/spiritual condition, family, country, and simply treating others with respect. I value these qualities immensely. Simply put, Mike walks the talk in all aspects of his life. I consider it a true honor to call Mike a friend.

ROSS VLIETSTRA

Mike Novakoski is a genuine leader with a passion for learning, growth, and continual improvement for both himself and his business. In a world where many leaders pay lip service to the principles they espouse, it is refreshing to deal with someone who truly lives by the values he promotes.

TIM MACK

Director, FJM Property
Perth, Australia

I met Mike ("Nova") ten years ago. During that time, we've encouraged each other as leaders of our individual companies, celebrated successes, and handled challenging periods. While our industries are different, his being construction and mine manufacturing, the challenges of operating a business are similar regardless of the industry.

While I've listened to Nova talk about E&V's employee-focused business and new employee onboarding activities, I only recently fully appreciated what Nova and Parker have built at E&V. Like many manufacturing companies, we've struggled to find and keep talented employees. In an effort to improve turnover issues, we are in the process of developing an effective onboarding process. I immediately thought of Nova and the processes utilized at E&V. I set up a visit to E&V with my key executives, asking Nova for about an hour of his time, and I was blown away. After not one, but three hours with Nova I realized our issue was about much more than onboarding. Nova described the culture at E&V, the subsequent successes, and the individual U-maps and team building activities E&V has embraced.

I'm confident that the incorporation of tools similar to those at E&V will address our turnover issues and allow our workforce to become more effective and fully engaged.

KEVIN BASSETT
President, Spectrum Decorative Finishes

As both a personal friend and trade contractor of Mike Novakoski, I can unequivocally say that Mike and his team at Elzinga & Volkers are a truly unique and special group of people. Their approach to everything from relations with their trade contract partners to project delivery methods to community outreach are innovative and distinguishing. Mike is a genuine and energetic person who engages in way that shows that he not only values the personal side of contractor relationship—friendship—but the unique trade talents that companies like Kent Companies bring to the marketplace. It's no wonder that Elzinga & Volkers are a perennial finalist for the American Subcontractor Association of Michigan's Michigan Contractor of the Year.

JEFF VANDERLAAN
CEO, Kent Companies

Elzinga & Volkers exemplifies the ideals of the Best and Brightest Program, focusing on better business and creating richer lives with leadership-driven results. Because they understand and implement continuous learning and measuring results for constant improvement, year over year they raise the bar of expectations and performance.

JENNIFER KLUGE

CEO, National Association for Business Resources

I thoroughly enjoyed working alongside Mike for several weeks this past year. He and his partners are passionate, focused, caring, and successful businesspeople with a great message that any firm could benefit from. Mike charismatically shares his success stories and people like myself are inspired to make continuous upgrades to our culture as a result. Mike and I both share a belief in the power of leading from the heart. I have seen incredible results first-hand in my own business! Mike is a focused leader who creates a true feeling of belonging for everyone. In a commodity industry like construction, Mike's approach to building an unmistakable culture has given E&V a level of success unattainable to 99 percent of his competition.

RACHANA SINGH

Owner and Director, JW Marriott Hotel/Synergy Thrislington
Chandigarh, India

When Lutheran Social Services Michigan (now Samaritas) looked for a contractor to reposition its state-wide campuses, we had three essential qualities [we were looking for]—integrity, commitment to our mission, and sensitivity to the seniors we served. Selecting E&V was the best decision we ever made.

REV. DR. LOUIS PRUES

Former Sr. Vice President of Development, Samaritas

Mike and his team at E&V have done the things I have aspired to do in my business. His approach to relationships with every stakeholder is authentic and grounded in doing the right thing. And it works. Talented people are line up to join E&V. Business owners are interested in learning from them. I was so inspired by Mike's approach that I decided to join him.

ROB DWORTZ
Former President/CEO/CHB, Bank of Holland

In *Becoming Unmistakable*, Mike and John share their inspiring story of transforming Elzinga & Volkers to be truly people focused. Their wisdom can be applied to any business, including those of us in the non-profit sector. I can't wait to apply the many lessons I learned to my own work and life.

JANE CLARK
President, West Coast Chamber of Commerce

I have had the opportunity to partner with Mike Novakoski and Elzinga & Volkers for the better part of twenty years and it has been wonderful to see such a transition in the company's culture. When Mike became president, we were able to notice subtle changes in the way we worked with our contacts. After a few years, those changes were no longer subtle, but rather a completely new way of doing business and communication had emerged. With a foundation of trust, true authority was given to employees to carry out their responsibilities … fostering an enviable culture of engaged employees.

Today, Elzinga & Volkers with their energy, employee-centric culture, and creativity is a company that we look to emulate … in my mind, the most powerful compliment one can give.

JOHN ROGERS
Principal, HNI

Novakoski's focus on team and people empowerment has created a strong culture of highly self-motivated team players at E&V. This leads to a significant competitive advantage in the construction industry. The ideas in this book show business leaders how important culture is to make one's own business stand out from the rest—becoming unmistakable.

GLEN CU

Managing Director, Lunar Steel Corporation
Pasig, Philippines

Over the past two decades, we have experienced one of our company's oldest and most valued suppliers transform itself!

P. J. THOMPSON

President and Chief Operating Officer, Trans-Matic Manufacturing

Mike and John have taken the basic human needs of appreciation and caring to a level that is unparalleled in an individualized industry. Their passion to push people to think outside of themselves and to help others brings those same people to a whole different level of giving and thus fulfills and builds their self-esteem and confidence. Being personally involved in discussions with these two men on ideas implemented from this book, I know their heart is focused on their company's number one asset: their people.

No matter the industry type you are in, this book works across the board and is much needed in a world that is so self-centered. It may seem like a daunting task to implement, but remember this was not done overnight and has taken years to achieve. We have implemented portions of this in our company, based upon its size, and have a group that is dedicated and would stick together no matter what we do.

JEFF SNAY

President, Pyramid Acoustics, Inc., and Prism Glass, Inc.

Mike Novakoski has used innovative approaches to creating an authentic, appreciative culture. Novakoski has many insights to help businesses promote a culture that is attractive to team members and trade partners, and stands out from the crowd.

MIKE DYKSTRA

President and CEO, Zeeland Lumber and Supply

Become Unmistakable gives inspiration to us right-brained leaders to use this charactcristic as our greatest asset, not an oddity to keep in the closet. Having a front row seat to watch Mike's joy in leading this transformation at EV has be an education in how to bring meaningful relationships and fun into the workplace.

ANDREW BOLT

President, Patten Monument Company

Michael has been a constant source of thought-provoking and innovative ideas. You and your career certainly will benefit, as I have, from the ideas in this book. His creative approach to employee engagement and unique business solutions has led to would class customer intimacy. The best part is that these ideas are transferable to your business!

DONZELL S. TAYLOR

President and CEO, Welty Building Company

Mike and John are the real deal. They live the principles outlined in this book. The change in their company's culture is palpable and exciting to witness. May we all have enough motivation to focus our energy on making our organizations unmistakable!

SHELLEYE YAKLIN

President and CEO, North Ottawa Community Health System

Mike and John have written an unmistakably helpful narrative for any business who is looking to positively change their businesses culture. Having worked with Mike for the last seven years as a business advisor, his leadership is unmatched and he challenges the status quo, is a selfless leader, and has immense compassion for his work and people. I've personally witnessed him promote his vision through empowering his team and culture. Great results have followed.

CARLYE KLIMEK, BDO
Tax Partner, USA LLP

Become Unmistakable: A Journey from Commodity to Oddity is like pulling back the curtain in *The Wizard of Oz*, an intimate look behind what makes one of West Michigan's Best and Brightest companies such a success. This book is a reflection on the unique beliefs and behaviors which make E&V unmistakably E&V!

MARK WILSON
Bank Executive

Every time I talk to Mike I leave with a renewed passion for building my company's culture and a few new ideas to put into practice! Mike is a fountain of passion and knowledge when it comes to building a company with an engaged team that really stands out from the competition. I have watched Mike and E&V for the last ten years and am consistently impressed with their ability to continuously increase the value given to customers, employees, and partners.

KEITH M. NIELSON
Principal, Generations Management, LLC

When I first met Mike I very quickly learned to listen and appreciate him for his benevolence and his desire to help people. He communicates his ideas simply and calmly; he is a true person and a true friend of mine.

THIERRY COSTES

CEO, Groupe Beaumarly

Paris, France

I had the privilege of becoming a friend and business associate [of] Mike Novakoski, "Nova," ten years ago. Little did I know that the newly anointed leader of Elzinga & Volkers, a mid-sized commercial contractor in Holland, Michigan, was about to unleash a new mindset for his company and start prototyping an "employee first" [mindset] to be used in any business or group. I use the term "business" loosely; you can apply his system to almost any group of people with a common goal. After you read this book and institute the easy-to-follow lessons, your company, business, group, or association will be on an amazing track for success. I would equate this to franchising your own business, not someone else's. There is no need to reinvent the wheel; follow this book and reinvent yourself.

RICH BUITENHUIS

Owner, Buitenhuis Building and Design, LLC

E&V exemplifies how expecting and helping employees to show up fully—with their humanity and creativity both welcomed and celebrated—makes the best possible business sense.

If you think there is an "either/or" choice between being an employee-focused business or being a business-focused business, read this story about E&V. Not only is there an "and" instead of an "either/or," but E&V's culture and business outperforms all the rest.

We all need to belong, to have a sense of meaning, to make a difference, to be seen and accepted as we are. The E&V story shows how listening to those needs and inviting them into the workplace, instead of asking employees to check them at the door, makes for a winning company and a company of winners.

If there's a future worthy of aspiring to, it's one in which a company like E&V is not an oddity (as they call themselves), but the norm.

TERRY PLOCHMAN
Former President and CEO, Plochman, Inc.

It has been incredible to watch how E&V has transformed their company. The construction industry is not where you would expect [to find] such forward-thinking processes like building relationships and company culture. E&V has been very strategic with their innovative ideas. They are not afraid to take an idea and run with it. The result has been that they have created a team that achieves outstanding results. E&V has received numerous prestigious awards, but their real value is in the corporate culture they have created and in their happy customers and employees. Congratulations to E&V for being willing to step out and try things a different way. Truly a winning approach!

MIKE ROGERS
CEO, Rogers and Willard, Inc.
Construction Manager and Developer

E&V's journey "from commodity to oddity" is fascinating, motivating, and heartwarming. *Becoming Unmistakable* describes the kind of workplace we would all love to enjoy: a place where [the] company's leaders are willing to share their feelings and encourage others to do the same. We owe Mike and John a debt of gratitude for sharing their story in a way that provides an inspiring, but practical, road map for other companies who want to create vibrant and very human workplace cultures.

MAUREEN REID

Independent Consultant, BoardWorks Consulting
Halifax, Nova Scotia

This compelling and insightful book details the remarkable success story behind E&V. Mike Novakoski is a creative and inclusive leader who has achieved huge success by focusing on a creative, right brain approach to his business. You will feel inspired to run—not walk—to incorporate these changes into your own company!

LESLIE ROUTHIER

YPO International Forum Committee

The passion that Novakoski and Parker demonstrate to their team translates into everything they do. We can all learn how to be unmistakably different in the best possible way for work and life. A powerful read from start to finish!

SHELBY MEYER

Networks Council Director, YPO

In "Become Unmistakable - A Journey from Commodity to Oddity," you will find the way to business success by treating people right. The book demonstrates what a big difference it makes when the workplace is treated as a community and a family. Novakoski's energy and commitment to this way of leadership is profound and inspirational for anybody who seeks to build better relationships and a better business.

JOSÉ FLORES

Abastecedora de Empacadoras y Rastros, Food Industry Supplier
Monterrey, Mexico

Having [had] a seat at E&V's peer exchange roundtable over several years, I've personally witnessed the development of their genuinely creative and uniquely positive employee-centric culture. As a strategic subcontractor partner, we've been the beneficiaries of their inspiring approach as we've sought to grow our own fully engaged and enthusiastic workforce with very positive results. Now, through *Become Unmistakable*, you too can discover the keys to unlocking your right-brain creative leadership thinking to further develop an organization where employees strongly desire to contribute their talents.

TIM ALBERS
CEO, Quality Air/Comfort Systems USA

Mike and John are true visionaries. They have successfully implemented major innovations in a very traditional industry, all while keeping their employees and supplier at the center of their success.

JENNIFER OWENS
President, Lakeshore Advantage

I have been the beneficiary of Michael's ideas and insights through our participation in the CEO roundtable for eight years. While there are many books and programs on leadership and management, Michael's provides a real-life example through his results. Taking it to the next level, he is impacting those outside of his organization by enthusiastically sharing the story of Elzinga & Volkers.

CHRISTOPHER ENGLE, LUTCF, CFP, CHFC, AEP
Managing Partner, Argus Financial Consultants

The innovative and inspirational approach Mike has taken to his employee first corporate culture has forced me to take a second look at my organization. Mike has developed a proven method based on a theory that "people want to be led and not managed" that has not only improved his corporate culture and employee engagement but has also driven results. I look forward to implementing portions of this into my organization.

BRIAN ACCOMANDO

SVP Product, DH Enterprise & Associates

This book is impossible to put down! I have to congratulate Mike Novakoski and John Parker for writing a highly readable and engaging book that demonstrates how a shift in mindset combined with a focus on people builds a flywheel of repeatable success. In Become Unmistakable, the authors communicate clearly and with authority their journey leading E&V through a monumental shift impacting their culture and way of doing business. For whatever reason, it is not unusual for CEOs and leaders to have a blind spot when it comes to their teams and their culture. Why is this? Are soft skills & right brain thinking too hard to grasp? Is it too uncomfortable? Did they skip that class at school? Was it never taught? The beliefs and observations of this company's leadership are NOT hard to understand! Their actions elevated the success of all constituents — their employees, the company and their clients — into a rare strata of performance where everybody wins. I admire the accomplishments that Mike and John have earned at E&V. Zero voluntary turnover? That is awesome! They inspire me to make my company better. This book gives me a lot of ideas and encouragement to be more purposeful in my activities to foster a more employee centric firm, advance our culture, and help our whole team to flourish.

THOMAS H. REYNOLDS

Region Chair, East Central U.S. / YPO Pittsburgh
CEO/President, Highway Equipment Company